SUCCESSFUL
Obedience Handling

■

The *NEW* Best Foot Forward

Barbara S. Handler

This book is dedicated to:

My dogs, who made it possible;
My students, who made it necessary.

Copyright 1991 by Barbara S. Handler
Original Copyright 1984 under the title *Best Foot Forward*.

Printed in the United States of America

Library of Congress Cataloging-in-Publication Data

Handler, Barbara S.
    Successful obedience handling: the new Best foot forward / by
Barbara S. Handler.
        p.   cm.
    Updated ed. of: Best foot forward. c1984.
    Includes index.
    ISBN 0-931866-51-0 (pbk.)
    1. Dogs—Obedience trials. 2. Dogs—Handling. 3. Dogs—Showing.
I. Handler, Barbara S. Best foot forward. II. Title.
SF425.7.H36   1991
636.7'088'8—dc20   90-19366
                                                                         CIP

ISBN 0-931866-51-0

Cover Design, Interior Design, Typography: *Shadow Canyon Graphics*
Cover Photo: *Kent and Donna Dannen*

C O N T E N T S

Obedience Trials

Obedience Trials are a sport and all participants should be guided by the principals of good sportsmanship both in and outside of the ring. The purpose of Obedience Trials is to demonstrate the usefulness of the pure-bred dog as a companion of man, not merely the dog's ability to follow specified routines in the obedience ring. While all contestants in a class are required to perform the same exercises in substantially the same way so that the relative quality of the various performances may be compared and scored, the basic objective of Obedience Trials is to produce dogs that have been trained and conditioned always to behave in the home, in public places, and in the presence of other dogs, in a manner that will reflect credit on the sport of Obedience. The performance of dog and handler in the ring must be accurate and correct and must conform to the requirements of these Regulations. However, it is also essential that the dog demonstrate willingness and enjoyment of its work, and that smoothness and naturalness on the part of the handler be given precedence over a performance based on military precision and peremptory commands.

American Kennel Club
Obedience Regulations
March 1, 1990

People show their dogs in obedience trials for many different reasons — to have a tangible reward (a ribbon, a trophy, a certificate) for all of the months that they have spent training; to compete for local awards and placements in national rating systems; for the fun and companionship

It is vital that you have a clear view of your goals before you enter your dog in an obedience trial. Setting your sights realistically involves understanding your dog's limitations and your own level of commitment of time and energy.

with both the dogs and the people; or for a personal sense of satisfaction. Whatever your reasons, it is vital that you have a clear view of your goals before you enter your dog in an obedience trial. Setting your sights realistically involves understanding your dog's limitations and your own level of commitment of time and energy.

A dog that can perform all of the required exercises is generally a delightful house pet. However, the fact that your dog comes when he is called and does not drag you down the street on his leash does not mean that either of you is necessarily ready to enter an obedience trial.

An obedience trial is a formal competition and an artificial situation; therefore, the exercises must be done in a particular manner. The rules for competition are spelled out in *Obedience Regulations,* available free from the American Kennel Club, 51 Madison Avenue, New York, New York 10010. Every potential exhibitor should be familiar with this small booklet. There are, however, some unwritten rules that do not appear in that publication, as well as many ideas about handling and show preparation developed by experienced participants over the years, that may prove helpful to both new and experienced exhibitors. These are the subject of this book.

This book will give you many ideas about handling and show preparation developed by experienced participants over the years. It is especially useful for the individual who trains alone, without the benefit of a class situation or the advice of an experienced instructor.

Successful Obedience Handling: The New Best Foot Forward is meant to serve as an aid to the person who is already familiar with the basic requirements for the obedience exercises — it is not a training manual to teach the dog how to perform the exercises. I have assumed that the reader has an understanding of each exercise and has attended at least one obedience trial as a spectator. If you cannot attend a show, you should be totally conversant with the *Regulations.* The book is designed to fit with any training program and is especially useful for the individual who trains alone, without the benefit of a class situation or the advice of an experienced instructor.

Major changes in dog obedience have occurred since 1984. Obedience is receiving closer attention and better support from the AKC. This book has incorporated information on how these changes affect exhibitors.

Major changes have taken place in our sport since *Best Foot Forward* (1984) was written. A full revision of the *Regulations* has been completed. A new Utility exercise has been added. The AKC has created a new division for "performance events," including obedience, field, herding, and more. Obedience has received closer attention and better support from the AKC. A program has been instituted to evaluate judges more stringently by reviewing their performances regularly and by requiring them to attend seminars offered by the AKC across the country to educate and inform both experienced and new judges. More realistic testing is helping to weed out people who are not prepared to be successful judges. These changes affect exhibitors and have been incorporated into this new book.

Because one of my original goals in writing *Best Foot Forward* was to aid the exhibitor who trains alone or in classes where the instructors are not experienced obedience competitors, I have added a section on proof-training (or proofing) for each exercise. I hope that by following my suggestions for proofing your dog, you can significantly increase your chances of qualifying by preparing for the odd things that happen at dog shows. The proofing ideas presented in this edition are based on what I do with my own dogs and on suggestions by those who attend my training classes. If any of these activities do not seem appropriate for you and your dog, discuss them with your instructor, or do not attempt them.

A section on proof-training your dog is included for each exercise. The proofing ideas are based on what I do with my own dogs and on suggestions by those who attend my training classes.

Equipment

Exhibitors in remote areas often have difficulty finding good obedience equipment. I therefore have provided at the end of this book a list of companies that sell training equipment through the mail. I do not endorse any particular vendors and personally order different items from different places.

Eligibility

Is your dog eligible for AKC obedience trials? The answer is yes, if you own a registered purebred of one of the AKC recognized breeds, and if the dog has not been artificially altered *in any manner not customary for its breed.* This means that it is okay to show your tail-less Pembroke Welsh Corgi, but not your tail-less Labrador Retriever, unless the Lab was born that way. If your dog has been noticeably surgically altered because of an accident, he may not compete. Ethically, he should be removed from competition if he has has any surgical alteration other than spaying, castration, or debarking,

Your dog is eligible for AKC obedience trials if you own a registered purebred of one of the AKC recognized breeds, and if the dog has not been artificially altered in any manner not customary for its breed.

There are two types of special registrations, both called Indefinite Listing Privilege or ILP. The first type can be obtained for dogs eligible for the Miscellaneous Class. The other type of ILP number is granted to an unregistered but obviously purebred dog. This type of dog must be neutered, and the owner must provide proof of neutering from a veterinarian. This represents an attempt on the part of the AKC to promote the training but not the breeding of such animals.

even if the results are not visible. Dogs that have been neutered and/or debarked are eligible to compete.

There are two types of special registrations, both called Indefinite Listing Privilege or ILP. The first type can be obtained for dogs eligible for the Miscellaneous Class. When a breed becomes newly popular in the United States, the national breed club may apply for AKC recognition. New breeds are first admitted to the Miscellaneous Class and can be shown in AKC events under certain conditions (e.g., they cannot become conformation champions) until sufficient numbers have been individually registered and shown in the Miscellaneous Class. These dogs *can* earn obedience titles using their ILP numbers. When enough have been registered and shown, they are moved into one of the seven conformation groups (working, herding, toys, etc.). Dogs of these Miscellaneous Group breeds must be individually registered with the AKC and must also be registered with their national breed club.

To obtain an ILP number for a dog of this group, you must submit an application with color photographs to the AKC, accompanied by the required pedigree information from the breeder. Each dog is considered individually, although there is usually little difficulty in securing a number for one of these rare breeds. The exception to this rule is the Border Collie, whose fanciers have adamantly refused to be moved into the herding group for many years, contending that they do not want their dogs bred for looks, but only for working ability. From time to time, Border Collie owners experience difficulty securing ILP numbers for their dogs, especially if the dogs bear marking other than the traditional black and white.

The other type of ILP number is granted to an unregistered but obviously purebred dog. This is often a dog that has been bought from a breeder of dubious credentials or rescued from the local animal shelter. The same rules apply in terms of making individual application for the ILP and providing color photographs of the dog. In addition, however, these animals *must* be neutered, and the owner must supply proof of neutering from a veterinarian. This represents a laudable attempt on the part of the AKC to promote the training but not the breeding of such animals.

If your dog does not meet these eligibility criteria, you can still show him to one or more titles. Mixed breeds, dogs that have been surgically altered, etc. can earn special titles by competing at fun matches. Write to the mixed-breed organizations listed at the back of this book for details.

Mixed breeds can earn special titles by competing at fun matches.

■

CHAPTER ONE

Is Your Dog Ready To Show?

Defining Your Goals

Success is a word that we each define differently. For one exhibitor, success may mean winning a placement in a class or achieving a particularly high score. The same handler, with a more difficult dog, may be thrilled simply to qualify and to have verification that the dog is truly under control. Some people are competitive by nature; others are not.

If you are going to enjoy the world of obedience training and exhibiting, you must set goals that are meaningful for *you*. Train to please yourself, and don't feel that you must have the same orientation to obedience exhibiting as any other person. You must also maintain a realistic perspective of your dog's abilities. It is fine to expect your dog to give you his best (assuming, of course, that you have done *your* best as a trainer), but not every dog is capable of achieving top scores. Be honest in your assessment, and be satisfied with your dog's best efforts, no matter what score he earns.

One Ultimate Goal — The Obedience Trial Championship (OTCh)

For those people who are exceptionally competitive and who have the time and money to devote to the sport, the OTCh is often considered the ultimate goal. Once a dog has earned his U.D., he may continue to compete in Open B and Utility B. If the dog is capable of winning those classes (and in many areas of the country, he will have to defeat a number of other OTCh dogs to win), he can become an Obedience Trial Champion.

If you are going to enjoy the world of obedience training and exhibiting, you must set goals that are meaningful for you. You must also maintain a realistic perspective of your dog's abilities.

For people who are competitive and who have the time and money to devote to the sport, the OTCh is often considered the ultimate goal.

Proof training means exposing the dog to as many possible distractions and strange situations as you can devise.

To accumulate points, the dog must win either first or second prize and must win at least three first prizes under three different judges. One of the firsts must be in Open B and one in Utility B; therefore, the dog must be good enough to win both classes. Wins at breed specialty shows do not count. The dog must earn a total of 100 points, based on the number of dogs that he defeats in a class. Not every dog is capable of OTCh-quality work, because the dog must be both sound and willing. Some trainers whiz through the OTCh with multiple dogs, taking only a handful of shows to achieve the goal, but the majority of us slog along for at least a year after earning the U.D., and some (author included) take more than a year. It is a proud moment indeed when the last points are finally earned.

Proof Training

There are several ways in which you can judge your dog's readiness to show before investing your fourteen to eighteen dollars in an entry fee. There are no guarantees, of course, but you can weigh the odds in your favor. Many trainers emphasize proof training for their canine students. Proof training means exposing the dog to as many possible distractions and strange situations as you can devise. For example, dogs can be proofed on the stay exercises with all kinds of noises, with food and squeaky toys being thrown near them, and with other dogs running loose while the dogs retain their positions. Check with your instructor about proofing on other exercises. If you train alone, you will have to be creative and ingenious about arranging for distractions. When you cannot trick your dog into making a mistake in training, it is probably time to move on. I will be talking more about proof training as we go on and will suggest ways to proof each exercise.

Pattern Training (Run-Throughs)

Many dogs also benefit — especially in the advanced classes — from pattern training. This means running your dog through all of the exercises in sequence, with no corrections, to assess his strengths and weaknesses. It can help both the handler and the dog to know what will come next. Some trainers object to pattern training on the grounds that it bores the dog. Ideally, pattern training is interspersed with work on individual exercises or parts of exercises.

Once the dog-and-handler team is secure in the performance of the individual exercises and of the entire set of exercises, it is time to begin attending matches.

Pattern training means running your dog through all of the exercises in sequence, with no corrections, to assess his strengths and weaknesses.

Matches

Matches are practice shows. They provide a training ground for dogs, handlers, judges, and show-giving clubs. They are also used as fund-raisers for clubs and other organizations. They are not always well organized, partly because the size of the entry is unpredictable. Plan to be there most of the day, especially if you are entering the Novice class. Matches provide a handler with the opportunity to learn some things about his or her dog.

Some behaviors with which you might want to experiment are:

Matches provide a training ground for dogs, handlers, judges, and show-giving clubs and provide a handler with the opportunity to learn some things about his or her dog. Plan to be there most of the day.

- How much warm-up time does my dog need to be sharp in the ring?
- When I am warming my dog up, will he resent or be crushed by a correction, or does he need a few pointed reminders of what I expect in the ring?
- Does my dog work better if he is isolated for an hour? Several hours?
- Does he need to be crated or in the car (if it is not too hot), or does he work better if kept on a down-stay at ringside?
- Does he require calming down or revving up just before we go in the ring to give his best performance?
- Does my dog work better if he is fed the morning of the show?
- Does "foreign" water give my dog diarrhea? If so, prepare to bring sufficient water from home to last all day.
- Can my dog perform the exercises to my satisfaction under simulated show conditions? If not, what are the weak points in our performance?

It is important to maintain your perspective regarding wins or losses at matches. While matches are very competitive in some areas of the country, in many other places they are meant only to provide opportunities for evaluation and correction.

It is important to maintain your perspective regarding wins or losses at matches. While matches are very competitive in some areas of the country, in many other places they are meant only to provide opportunities for evaluation and correction. Wins at matches have no real significance except for non-registerable dogs. Most match judges are sincerely trying to do a good job, but, like you and your dog, they are at the match to learn. Some match judges are inexperienced and ill-informed about the *Regulations*. Their scores are often wildly erratic — either much too high or much too low. They have been known to invent their own versions of the *Regulations*. Any advice offered the beginning handler by such judges should be verified with someone whose reliability and accuracy the handler is sure of.

In most areas of the country, dogs that have completed their titles should not be entered in those same level classes competitively. That is, a dog that has earned his C.D. should be entered in the Novice class "For Exhibition Only" and should not be eligible for any prizes or awards. It is often useful to enter an advanced dog in the Novice class to polish heeling or to deal with loss of confidence. It is also generally acceptable to show a dog "For Exhibition Only" if you wish to run him through the Open or Utility classes with the jumps set lower than would be required at an AKC trial. Furthermore, if you know in advance that your dog will need a double command or a correction on a particular exercise, it is appropriate to so advise the judge. The judge will generally permit this assistance but should automatically fail the dog for the exercise. That's fine — the point of going to the match was not necessarily to qualify, but rather to make the dog understand that he must perform the exercises in the way you require.

There are two types of matches: sanctioned and non-sanctioned (also called "fun" or "correction" matches). These may be open to all breeds or may be limited to only certain breeds. They may involve either conformation or obedience or both.

There are two types of matches: sanctioned matches and non-sanctioned matches (also called "fun" or "correction" matches). These may be open to all breeds to may be limited to only certain breeds. They may involve either conformation or obedience or both.

Sanctioned Matches

Sanctioned matches are run like AKC shows. They are limited to purebred dogs of recognized breeds, and no physical correction is permitted in the obedience rings. Dogs may receive verbal correction, and, at the discretion of the judge, exercises may be repeated.

Sanctioned matches are held by clubs attempting to meet AKC requirements for holding regular shows and obedience trials. They also serve as a training ground for new judges, who are required to officiate at a certain number of such matches to be eligible to judge at AKC obedience trials. Non-regular classes (other than Novice, Open, and Utility) may be offered, according to the needs of the area. Some sanctioned matches require pre-entry, and some are restricted to dogs that have only earned certain titles (for example, no dog that has earned a U.D. may compete). The advertising flyers should provide this information.

Sanctioned matches are limited to purebred dogs of recognized breeds, and no physical correction is permitted in the obedience rings. Dogs may receive verbal correction, and, at the discretion of the judge, exercises may be repeated.

Fun Matches

Fun matches may be organized in a number of different ways. There may be separate rings for the group exercises and non-regular classes such as sub-novice, graduate novice, brace, or just-for-fun classes such as mixed-braces (Newfoundlands and Papillons, for example), or trade-handler classes may be offered. Reasonable physical correction is permitted. Some people find it useful to enter the dog twice, either in the same class or in both the "A" and "B" sections of the class. The first time through, no corrections are given so that the dog's level of performance can be assessed. The second time through, corrections or help can be given to ease the dog over the rough spots or to prevent repetition of mistakes.

New types of fun matches are being seen around the country. These include "show-and-go" matches, which permit the handler to be judged on the individual exercises, to join a stay-group in a separate ring, and to receive his score sheet and leave, without waiting for the entire class to be judged. Such matches are non-competitive and are very handy for the exhibitor who wants to show several dogs or who has a limited amount of time to spend at the match. Some clubs provide working or practice rings in addition to regular exhibition rings. The participant buys a block of time, usually ten or fifteen minutes, in one of these rings. A match judge is available

In fun matches, reasonable physical correction is permitted. Some people find it useful to enter the dog twice. The first time through, no corrections are given so that the dog's level of performance can be assessed. The second time through, corrections or help can be given to ease the dog over the rough spots or to prevent repetition of mistakes.

to call commands or to offer assistance or advice for solving training problems.

When your dog has performed to your satisfaction at several matches and has shown himself capable of qualifying with some degree of consistency, it is time to enter him in a licensed obedience trial.

Final Thoughts on Readiness

It is beneficial to both dog and handler to wait until they are reasonably confident before entering an AKC trial. Readiness varies based on the dog's individual character and on the class entered.

Unless you live in an area where there are very few shows available, it is beneficial to both dog and handler to wait until they are reasonably confident before entering an AKC trial. Be aware, however, that readiness varies based on the dog's individual character and on the class entered. Many dogs can become so steady on the Novice exercises that they have a 90 to 95 percent likelihood of qualifying. Somewhat fewer dogs can reach that level of steadiness when they begin showing in Open (although many achieve it while showing in Open B). Utility is another matter. Because of the complexity of the behaviors required of the dog, very few dogs reach those high levels of reliability. The dog's understanding of the exercises seems to come and go without warning ("the fall-aparts"), even when they have been trained and shown in this class for long periods of time. It seems that luck has a powerful hand in determining the percentage of qualifying scores in the Utility class.

■

Entering A Licensed Trial

Judging the Judge

It is advisable to find out who will be judging the class that you intend to enter. Many judges run training classes, and their students may not show under those judges. This does not apply to a judge who puts on a brief training clinic in your area, but rather to the judge whose classes you attend on a regular basis. If you stop attending classes run by a judge, you must wait a year before showing your dog under that judge.

As you attend matches and trials, you will begin to hear stories — occasionally tales of horror — about various judges. You would do well to investigate further before giving credence to such rumors. There are certainly incompetent, capricious, and unpleasant obedience judges loose in the community, and you may indeed wish to avoid entering classes over which they are officiating. However, one disgruntled exhibitor does not a bad judge make. If you hear a negative story about a particular judge, ask several experienced people to verify it. Remember, judges have bad days, and they make mistakes like anyone else. Furthermore, some exhibitors have an inflated opinion of their dog's ability and may resent the truly observant judge who catches every error and scores dog and handler accordingly. If several different people have confirmed a particular judge's incompetence or unpleasant behavior, you may be wise to consider entering a different class (see page 8) or passing up that particular trial.

It is advisable to find out who will be judging the class that you intend to enter. Also, try to secure information about the trial site before sending in your entry. Try to learn about the type of surface on which you will be working.

The Trial Site

It is also advisable to try to secure some information about the trial site before sending in your entry. Will obedience be held indoors or outdoors? (Be aware that some indoor all-breed shows designate certain classes to be held outdoors.) If your dog has only been trained outdoors, you would do well to expose him to walking on rubber mats and near different types of ring enclosures (ropes, baby gates, curtains), and to working in a noisy building before entering an indoor trial. Some trial sites locate the obedience rings near the building entrance or near the snack bar. If your dog is somewhat shy, or has special problems with distractability, these trials may be more than he can handle.

You should also try to learn about the type of surface on which you will be working. Some trials are held on loose dirt (in horse barns, for example), which is hard for short-legged dogs to handle. There are outdoor trials held on hot asphalt, which is especially painful for dogs without much coat. Ask your instructor or a more experienced exhibitor for information. You can also contact the trial-giving club and ask questions about the site (the club secretary's address will appear in the Premium List).

Physically disabled exhibitors are welcome to compete at AKC obedience trials if they can get around the ring without the assistance of another person. Disabled exhibitors' dogs must perform all parts of every exercise, but judges are usually most helpful in accommodating to the disability. It is vital that people with mobility limitations investigate both the accessibility of the trial site and the floor surface of the obedience rings.

Handicapped Handlers

Physically disabled exhibitors are welcome to compete at AKC obedience trials if they can get around the ring without the assistance of another person. Judges or stewards will guide visually impaired persons between exercises. Deaf people who have difficulty with oral communication might want to bring along an interpreter who will not be allowed to enter the ring with the deaf person, but who can assist the exhibitor in establishing some system of signals to be used by the judge.

Disabled exhibitors' dogs must perform all parts of every exercise, but judges are usually most helpful in accommodating to the disability. Some outstanding dogs have been trained and handled by wheelchair-bound exhibitors who have competed successfully with able-bodied handlers. It is, of course, absolutely vital that people with mobility limitations investigate both the ac-

It is appropriate for the disabled handler and judge to establish heel position before starting the heeling.

cessibility of the trial site and the floor surface of the obedience rings. Even if you can bring your wheelchair into the building, you are not likely to do well if the ring surface is loose dirt or damp tanbark.

Filling Out the Entry Form

You must use an official AKC entry form to enter an AKC trial. These forms are included in the Premium List, which is published at least a month before the date of the show. The Premium List tells the exhibitor who is judging, which classes are offered, and which trophies and prizes (if any) are offered. It also gives the name and address of the show site and directions to it. You can obtain Premium Lists from the organizations that put on dog shows (known as show superintendents), or by writing to the trial-giving club (whose address can be

The Premium List tells the exhibitor who is judging, which classes are offered, and which trophies and prizes (if any) are offered. It also gives the name and address of the show site and directions to it.

OFFICIAL AMERICAN KENNEL CLUB ENTRY FORM
Dog Show & Obedience Trial

FLATIRONS KENNEL CLUB, INC.

Boulder County Fairgrounds   95th & Nelson Road   Longmont, Colorado

SATURDAY, MAY 26, 1984

ENTRY FEE (including 50 cent AKC recording fee) is $12.00 for the first entry of each dog except Puppy, Novice (Breed) & Bred-by-Exhibitor Classes which are $8.00. Each additional entry of the same dog is $8.00. When a dog is entered in more than one class, the highest priced class is considered the first entry. Junior Showmanship Competition is $4.00. Veteran Classes are $12.00.
ENTRIES CLOSE WEDNESDAY NOON, MAY 9, 1984 at Superintendents Office.
MAIL ENTRIES with Fees Payable to JACK ONOFRIO, SUPERINTENDENT,
Post Office Box 25764, Oklahoma City, Oklahoma 73125.

NOTICE: PLEASE PUT BREED & NAME OF SHOW ON CHECK.   I ENCLOSE $ .12 ....for entry fees

	OFFICE USE ONLY	SC			Bd			S
CL 1		CL 2		OB 1	OB 2	JS		O

IMPORTANT — Read carefully instructions on Reverse Side Before Filling Out. Numbers in the boxes indicate sections of the instructions relevant to the information needed in that box. (PLEASE PRINT)

BREED Belgian Tervuren	VARIETY [1]	SEX Dog

DOG [2] [3]
SHOW
CLASS

CLASS [3]
DIVISION
Weight color etc

ADDITIONAL CLASSES	OBEDIENCE TRIAL CLASS Novice B	JR SHOWMANSHIP CLASS

NAME OF (See Back)
JUNIOR HANDLER (if any)

FULL NAME OF DOG   Ch. Fern Hill Act One

X AKC REG NO Enter number here WD365671	DATE OF BIRTH 04-12-76
□ AKC LITTER NO	
□ ILP NO	PLACE OF [XX] U S A □ Canada □ Foreign
□ FOREIGN REG NO & COUNTRY	BIRTH Do not print the above in catalog

BREEDER   Barbara S. Handler

SIRE   Ch. Icarus de Sharrvonne C.D.

DAM   Ch. Xquisite de Braise Rouge U.D. T.

ACTUAL OWNER(S)   Barbara S. Handler
[4]   (PLEASE PRINT)
OWNER'S ADDRESS   100 Any Road
CITY   Anytown   STATE   CO   ZIP   80000

NAME OF OWNER'S AGENT   CODE #
(IF ANY) AT THE SHOW

I CERTIFY that I am the actual owner of the dog, or that I am the duly authorized agent of the actual owner whose name I have entered above. In consideration of the acceptance of this entry. I (we) agree to abide by the rules and regulations of The American Kennel Club in effect at the time of this show or obedience trial, and by any additional rules and regulations appearing in the premium list for this show or obedience trial or both, and further agree to be bound by the "Agreement" printed on the reverse side of this entry form. I (we) certify and represent that the dog entered is not a hazard to persons or other dogs. This entry is submitted for acceptance on the foregoing representation and agreement.

SIGNATURE of owner or his agent
duly authorized to make this entry _____ TELEPHONE # 666-666-6666

A sample entry form. Be sure to sign the form, indicate the correct division as well as class, and include the entry fee.

obtained by writing to the AKC). A list of dog-show superintendents can be found at the back of this book. Trial dates and locations are listed regularly in *Pure Bred Dogs, American Kennel Gazette* (known to its intimates as *The Gazette*). This monthly magazine is frequently available at your local public library, or you can subscribe to it by writing to the AKC at the address provided in the Introduction. *The Gazette* is now sold in three sections: "Pure-Bred Dogs" (contains articles, breed club columns, and news of official AKC business), "Awards" (lists titles earned and all show, obedience, herding, and field trial results), and "Events" (lists all upcoming AKC events for the next three to five months). You may subscribe to any or all of these sections.

The Gazette *is frequently available at your local public library, or you can subscribe to it by writing to the AKC. The Gazette is sold in three sections: "Pure-Bred Dogs," "Awards," and "Events."*

If you attend several shows or trials put on by the same dog-show organization, your name will be put on its mailing list, and you will receive Premium Lists for all of the local shows and trials that use the services of that superintendent. You can also telephone the office of the superintendent for information about the trial site, entry fees, closing date, etc. Most of the major superintendents now have facilities to accept entries by telephone or fax machine if you have a major credit card.

Many obedience clubs do not use the services of a show superintendent, so you must contact the club directly to obtain its Premium List.

Many obedience clubs do not use the services of a show superintendent, so you must contact the club directly to obtain its Premium List. You can use an entry blank from any official Premium List to enter a different trial. Simply cross out the preprinted name, location, and date and write in the information for the trial that you wish to enter. If you are unsure of the entry fee, you might want to send a check for a few dollars more than the average entry fee in your area. The excess will be refunded to you by mail or at the show.

Be certain to fill out all of the spaces on the entry form, and copy the information exactly as it appears on your dog's AKC registration slip. A sample entry form can be found on page 16. Study it carefully before filling out your first entry form. Be certain that the form is legible; typing the information is ideal. You may use a pre-printed return address label (the kind you buy to use on your letters) in the section marked "Actual Owner(s)." If your name and address are not readable, you may not get the judging schedule and your entry information back before the day of the trial.

Be certain to fill out all of the spaces on the entry form, and copy the information exactly as it appears on your dog's AKC registration slip.

Which Class — "A" or "B"?

Certain classes are restricted to certain dogs and handlers. Following is a list of the classes and the rules for entering each.

Novice A

Novice A is for the new exhibitor with his or her first dog. You may only show a dog that you own or co-own, or that is owned by a member of your immediate family. Novice B is for all other Novice dogs, including those that you are training for another person.

This class is for the new exhibitor with his or her first dog. You may only show a dog that you own or co-own, or that is owned by a member of your immediate family. *Beware: if you (a new exhibitor) co-own a dog with another person, and that person has put even ONE obedience title on any other dog, the dog that you co-own is ineligible for Novice A — even if the co-owner has never trained the dog in question.* The AKC has no way of knowing who trained the dog. You may show only one dog to a C.D. in Novice A; any subsequent dogs that you train must be shown in Novice B. If you have trained two dogs simultaneously, you may enter only one in Novice A (if he is eligible), but you may enter the other in Novice B.

Novice B

This class is for all other Novice dogs, including those that you are training for another person.

Open A

In Open A, you may show as many dogs as you like as long as you are the owner or co-owner of record and have not earned an Obedience Trial Championship (O.T.Ch.) on any other dog.

This class is for all dogs that have confirmed Companion Dog (C.D.) titles, handled by the owners, co-owners, or their immediate families. Many people misunderstand Open A: unlike Novice A, *you may show as many dogs as you like in this class, as long as you are the owner or co-owner of record and have not earned an Obedience Trial Championship (O.T.Ch.) on any other dog.*

Open B

Once your dog's Companion Dog Excellent (C.D.X.) title has been confirmed, you may continue to show him indefinitely in Open B. In addition, Open B is the class for Open dogs not owned by their handlers and for all Open dogs owned or co-owned by judges and by people who have previously earned an Obedience Trial Championship on another dog.

Utility A

This class has the same restrictions as Open A. The dogs must be owner-handled and must not have confirmed U.D. titles.

Utility B

This is the counterpart to Open B. In the past, Utility was not always divided into A and B sections. As of January 1, 1990, however, all clubs must offer both Utility A and Utility B.

"A" Versus "B"

In general, the competition for high scores and class placements is less keen in the "A" classes than in the "B" classes. The handling is less polished, and the dogs are usually not as steady. This can be important if you have a dog with stay problems that is easily lured out of position by other dogs' misbehavior.

The group exercises in the "B" classes are usually — not always — less chaotic. If your dog is ineligible for "A" classes because of ownership, or if the judge is one under whom you have already earned a qualifying score, you may always choose to enter the "B" class; it is unrestricted. If you mistakenly show your dog in an "A" class when he is ineligible, the AKC will eventually discover the error (it may take several months) and will notify you that the dog's title, if any, is rescinded and that all awards made to your dog are cancelled. Any ribbons and trophies must be returned to the clubs that awarded them, and you must start all over in the correct class.

Open B is for Open dogs not owned by their handlers and for all Open dogs owned or co-owned by judges and by people who have previously earned an Obedience Trial Championship on another dog.

Dogs in Utility A must be owner-handled and must not have confirmed U.D. titles.

Utility B is the counterpart to Open B. As of January 1, 1990, all clubs must offer both Utility A and Utility B.

Competition for high scores and class placement is less keen in the "A" classes than in the "B" classes. The handling is less polished, and the dogs are usually not as steady.

About seven to ten days before the show or trial, you will receive a judging schedule or program in the mail. This will give you the time that your class begins, the number of dogs entered in each class, and the number of the ring in which your class will be held.

The Judging Schedule: When Should I Arrive?

About seven to ten days before the show or trial, you will receive a judging schedule or program in the mail. This will give you the time that your class begins, the number of dogs entered in each class, and the number of the ring in which your class will be held. There will also be either a copy of your entry form with your armband number written in, or a printed card (an entry ticket) listing your dog's name and your assigned armband number. This ticket may also be used as an admission pass to the hall or fairgrounds where the trial will be held.

Given this information, you can calculate approximately what time you will show. For example, the schedule might say, "Novice A — 8:00 a.m. — #'s 020-075." If your armband number is 037, you will be the seventeenth exhibitor in a class of fifty-five dogs. Classes are generally judged at the following rates:

Novice: eight dogs per hour

Open: seven dogs per hour

Utility: six dogs per hour

Therefore, you would be likely to show a little after 10:00 a.m. However, this is only a rough estimate and should be used with caution. Half of the dogs ahead of you may be absent, particularly if the weather is bad or if the trial is the last of several on the same weekend. Also, some judges seem to feel a personal challenge to be finished first and therefore run their rings like races.

Refunds

You cannot show a bitch in season in the obedience ring. If your bitch comes in season after the entries have closed, some clubs will refund your entry fee. Check the Premium List. If the club is forced to change judges after the entries have closed, you may also request a refund, in writing, before the day of the trial, from the superintendent or trial secretary, or you may submit your withdrawal at the show (if you were planning to attend anyway) no later than thirty minutes before *any* obedience judging starts. Generally, your refund will be mailed to you within a few weeks.   ∎

CHAPTER THREE

Trial Day Arrives

Looking Like a Pro

Your Dog

The way you and your dog look at a trial makes a statement about you. You have put a great deal of time into training your dog. Now, spend an extra hour or two on his grooming to show the world that you are proud of him. No matter how far your dog is from the ideal described in the breed standard, you owe it to him to groom him as though he were a breed champion (and if he *is* a breed champion, it is even more important that he be presented looking his best).

This means checking that his nails are cut short, that his coat is clean and free of mats, and that he is trimmed (if that is appropriate for his breed). Your dog may be the only representative of his breed that the public sees, and the way he looks will affect their impression of the entire breed.

Judges cannot help but be impressed by a smartly groomed dog and handler. This should not affect the dog's score, but your joint appearance sets the tone for your performance in the ring. Furthermore, no judge should have to handle a dirty dog.

The Handler

Now that the dog is spruced up, it is time to look at the handler. Obedience is not a contact sport, and there is no reason for any handler to appear in the ring in old jeans and a worn-out t-shirt. Show respect for

A wonderful outfit for turning over the compost pile, but totally inappropriate for an obedience trial.

An improvement, but not very practical if you want a dog to see where he's going. Dress nicely, but sensibly.

Ready to show!
The way you and your dog look at a trial makes a statement. Judges cannot help but be impressed by a smartly groomed dog and handler.

yourself and your dog by dressing nicely. Think about the colors and styles you wear, because they may have an influence on the dog's performance. It is not a bad idea to wear pants and shoes the same color as your dark-colored dog. It occasionally makes the slightly crooked sit less noticeable. If you are going to use hand signals in the ring, consider wearing a light-colored shirt and a dark jacket so that your clothing will contrast with your surroundings, giving the dog a better chance of seeing your arm movements. If the building is very dark, you can expose the light-colored garments and vice-versa.

Wear comfortable shoes with rubber soles. Noisy boots or wooden clogs can make enough noise to be construed as an additional signal to the dog on the heeling exercise, causing points to be deducted.

A woman who wishes to wear a skirt or dress in the ring should be certain that it does not hit the dog in the face. She should wear a skirt while practicing, because some dogs are not used to seeing material flapping between themselves and the handler. For the same reason, it is wise to avoid wearing dangling jewelry. Men should wear tie tacks to keep their ties from flapping at the dog, especially when taking a retrieved article.

Showing small dogs or short-legged dogs requires extra forethought by the handler. Proper footwear is especially important, because feet loom so large to the small dog. Avoid wide-legged pants that will flap in the dog's face and force him out of heel position.

Equipment

Collars

The *Regulations* spell out the types of collars and leashes that are acceptable in the obedience ring. Plain, buckle collars, or slip collars of fabric, leather, or chain may be used. The *Regulations forbid* slip collars that *also* have a snap or a buckle, or that have more than two rings. You may *not* have a pinch or prong collar on your dog if the dog is entered in an obedience class. This regulation has caused some real confusion, because it is apparently acceptable to have a pinch collar on a dog

Note: You cannot wear any clothing or jewelry in the ring with the name of a particular kennel or dog-related club. Similarly, in Utility your article container should not advertise your dog's name and trial record. Obedience trials are to be an anonymous contest.

Show respect for yourself and your dog by dressing nicely. Think about the colors and styles you wear, because they may have an influence on the dog's performance.

Wear comfortable shoes with rubber soles. Avoid wearing dangling jewelry, flapping ties, and wide-legged pants.

Plain, buckled collars, or slip collars of a single length of fabric, leather, or chain may be used. The Regulations *forbid slip collars that also have a snap or a buckle, or that have more than two rings.*

These are unacceptable *collars for the obedience ring. Clockwise, from upper left: a pinch or prong collar (euphemistically referred to in the* Regulations *as a "special training collar"); a fancy buckle collar with rhinestones; although it is hard to see in the photo, this collar has a clip rather than a buckle and is forbidden (it might also be considered "fancy" because it has little sheep on it); this slip collar has a clip on one end, not the required rings; this leather collar has a tag attached and bears the dog's name, thereby identifying the dog (the tooled leather might also be considered "fancy" by some judges, even if the name were not present).*

These are acceptable *collars. Clockwise from upper left: a snake or jewel choke collar (also known as a slip collar); a nylon buckle collar; a plain leather buckle collar; a nylon choke collar; a metal choke chain.*

A poorly fitted choke or slip collar.

Now we add a heavy leash with a large snap, and it is a wonder the dog can walk at all.

A properly fitted buckle collar.

entered in conformation (and some dogs are so untrained that they need these collars badly); however, the obedience dogs cannot wear them on the grounds of a show, trial, or sanctioned match. I suggest that you keep any such equipment well away from the obedience rings.

The collar should fit properly and not be so tight that it makes an indentation in the dog's neck, or so loose that the dog looks as though he could step through the collar at any moment. Owners of small dogs are the worst

The collar should not be so tight that it makes an indentation in the dog's neck or so loose that the dog looks as though he could step through the collar at any moment.

offenders, often bringing toy dogs into the ring with collars so big that the dogs trip over them. There must not be any tags hanging from the collar.

Leashes

Leashes may be of leather or fabric (not chain or plastic) and must only be long enough to allow for slack in the Heel on Leash. The collar and leash must be separate.

Leashes may be of leather or fabric (not chain or plastic) and must only be long enough to allow for slack in the Heel on Leash. There is no regulation requiring a six-foot leash. The collar and leash must be separate. I once judged a man with a fluffy-coated Afghan, who surprised me at the end of the Figure 8 by slipping off the entire nylon show-lead, leaving the dog collarless. I sent him out to find a correct collar and leash and finished judging him later. The leash may be hooked to either or both rings of the slip collar.

Other Supplies

Sample Supply List
- *Dog crate.*
- *Treats or toys.*
- *Container of water.*
- *Drinking bowl.*
- *Spare collars/leashes.*
- *Grooming equipment.*
- *Towel or rug.*
- *Folding chair.*
- *Lunch.*
- *Dumbbells.*
- *Scent discrimination articles.*
- *Rain gear.*
- *Extra towels.*
- *Ice (for hot weather).*
- *Sheets or silvered blankets that reflect the sun.*
- *Medical supplies.*

You would do well to make and keep a list of the equipment that you need and to check things off as you load the car to go to the trial. Your list is likely to include a dog crate, treats or toys (if you use them), a container of water, a drinking bowl, spare collars and leashes in case one breaks, grooming equipment, a towel or rug for the dog to lie on, a folding chair (unavailable at most outdoor trials), and your lunch (the food usually sold at dog shows is notoriously inedible). You may have other items to add to the list, including dumbbells and scent discrimination articles. Dog equipment vendors are often present at dog shows (less frequently at separate obedience trials), so you may be able to fill in any gaps at the trial.

If you will be attending an outdoor trial, be aware that bad weather is no reason to stop a dog show. Carry rain gear, including extra towels to keep the dog reasonably dry. Judges will also be wearing rain gear, so it is a good idea to accustom your dog to working around someone wearing a rustling rain poncho, carrying an umbrella, and (since the weather isn't always bad), wearing a floppy sun hat. This is part of the proofing process discussed earlier.

You must also keep your dog cool in the heat. Some

trial sites have little or no shade. Some people carry extra ice to put in the bottom of the dog's crate. You can turn a metal crate pan upside down and put several blocks of *Blue Ice*® underneath (be careful, however, that the dog cannot reach the *Blue Ice*®; it contains poisonous anti-freeze). Many exhibitors provide shade for the dogs by covering the tops of exercise pens or crates with sheets or, preferably, silvered blankets that reflect the sun.

If you are traveling any distance from home, you should include some medical supplies with your eqipment. An anti-diarrheal preparation such as *Kaopectate*® or *Pepto Bismol*®, preferably in tablets rather than messy liquid form, is indispensable. If your dog tends to have digestive problems away from home, check with your vet about a more powerful medication that you can carry on trips. Take an adequate supply of any regular medication that your dog requires. There is a veterinarian on call at every show or trial. If your dog is injured or becomes ill, you can ask the club to call the vet. You will be expected to pay for the vet's services in most instances.

There is a veterinarian on call at every show or trial. You will be expected to pay for vet's services that you may require in most instances.

At the Trial

It is generally a good idea to arrive at least two hours before your dog is scheduled to show. This allows time for you to get lost on the way, find the parking area, unload your paraphernalia, and find your ring, while still giving the dog time to settle. By attending matches, you have learned how much settling time your dog requires to do his best in the ring. Take this into account when planning your arrival time. The class cannot begin before the published time, but judges do not have to permit latecomers to exhibit. If you are unavoidably late (a flat tire or other real disaster), apologize to the judge and stewards and inquire if you have been marked absent. If not, the judge will tell you when you may show — often at the end of the class.

At a large, all-breed show, it is easy to become confused on the show grounds. Obedience rings are usually clustered together and are often separated from the breed rings. If the rings are not numbered consecutively, look for the rings with the jumps.

Arrive at least two hours before your dog is scheduled to show. The class cannot begin before the published time, but judges do not have to permit latecomers to exhibit. If you are unavoidably late, apologize to the judge and stewards and inquire if you have been marked absent. If not, the judge will tell you when you may show — often at the end of the class.

Soon after you arrive, buy a catalogue.

The Catalogue

Soon after you arrive, it is a good idea to buy a catalogue. This is a small book listing the names and addresses of all the exhibitors as well as the dogs' registered names. You will find the obedience listings at the back of the catalogue. Obedience dogs are generally shown in the order in which their names are printed ("catalogue order"). If you have a problem with showing in catalogue order, such as a conflict with another ring, you should approach the judge before the class begins and request to show earlier or later. The judge is *not* required to permit this, but most are accommodating if the request is polite and reasonable. Similarly, if you are showing two dogs in the same class, the judge may permit you to put them in different stay groups if you do not have an extra handler. Again, *this is the judge's choice, not his or her obligation,* and the judge may deny your request. If that happens, you may have to choose between two classes and forfeit one entry.

I do not believe that judges should penalize exhibitors for showing in conformation and obedience or for showing more than one dog. I think that judges should always try to accommodate the exhibitor. However, some people abuse this opportunity, hoping to give their dog some advantage by showing earlier or later than their scheduled time. For this reason, many judges are reluctant to alter the established order of showing.

Check to see that your name is listed in the correct class. If your name does not appear, or if it is listed in an incorrect class, take your entry ticket to the show superintendent, who will have a large table in some prominent place, or to the trial secretary, and ask that the problem be corrected.

Check to see that your name is listed in the correct class. If your name does not appear, or if it is listed in an incorrect class, take your entry ticket to the show superintendent or trial secretary and ask that the problem be corrected.

If everything is in order, look at the front of the obedience listings and read about the various trophies or prizes being offered. There may be a prize offered for the highest scoring dog of a breed, or of a group, for which you are eligible. In some cases, you must register for certain prizes at the trophy table or at your ring. These include trophies for people living in a certain geographical area, for junior handlers (under eighteen), for seniors (over fifty or fifty-five), etc.

Special Awards

In addition to winning awards at shows, you may also compete for some special awards that are national in scope.

AKC Obedience Titles

When your dog has qualified in the same class at three shows, under three different judges, the AKC will automatically send you a certificate and publish your dog's name in the *Gazette*. You do not have to apply for your certification. If you have not received your certificate within two months of your third qualifying score, contact the AKC Show Records Department by telephone or by mail to verify your qualifying scores. Many people like to earn an extra qualifying score (a security leg) in case an earlier score was somehow lost in the computer records. You may continue to show your dog in either Novice class or in Open A or Utility A for thirty days after you and the dog have received your third qualifying score.

When your dog has qualified in the same class at three shows, under three different judges, the AKC will automatically send you a certificate and publish your dog's name in the Gazette. *You may continue to show your dog in either Novice class or in Open A or Utility A for thirty days after you and the dog receive your third qualifying score.*

The DOG WORLD Award

Dog World magazine will print your dog's name and picture and will send you a certificate if your dog qualifies for any degree in his first three trials (no failures) with scores of 195 or better. You must write to the magazine to inform them of your eligibility. *Dog World* can be purchased at many newsstands.

Dog World *magazine will print your dog's name and picture and will send you a certificate if your dog qualifies for any degree in his first three trials with scores of 195 or better.*

The Ratings Systems

The Delaney System

This system counts the number of dogs that your dog has defeated by winning class placements or Highest Scoring Dog in Trial. You earn one point for every dog that you defeat. Information is taken from show results published in the *Gazette*, and winners' names and dogs'

The Delaney System counts the number of dogs that your dog has defeated by winning class placements or Highest Scoring Dog in Trial.

names for every breed are published in *Front and Finish*, a monthly national obedience newspaper (P.O. Box 333, Galesburg, Illinois 61401).

The Shuman System

The Shuman System awards points to dogs that earn qualifying scores in Open and Utility classes (not Novice).

This system awards points to dogs that earn qualifying scores in Open and Utility classes (not Novice). The higher the score, the more points you are awarded. Results are automatically published in *Front and Finish*. Winners are notified in advance that they have placed in the system (but are not told what their ranking is) so that they can send a picture of their dog, which will be published along with the listings. Notice that both of these systems recognize dogs by individual breed and by groups, as well as acknowledge the top ten dogs overall. Placing in either of these systems is an honor.

Breed Club System

Many national breed clubs also rate dogs of their breed in obedience. Most publish their results in their national publication and/or notify winners by mail.

Many national breed clubs also rate dogs of their breed in obedience. They use many different systems, and most will publish their results in their national publication and/or notify winners by mail. Some clubs also have traveling trophies that the winner may keep for a year and then pass on to the next winner.

Sportsmanship

Sportsmanship implies courtesy to judges and to competing exhibitors and gentle treatment of the dog.

Now that you and your dog are on the trial grounds, there are some things that you should and should not do. The AKC requires all exhibitors to conduct themselves in a sportsmanlike manner and backs up that expectation by giving show-giving clubs the power to suspend exhibitors' privileges to compete in AKC events. Sportsmanship in this case implies courtesy to judges and to competing exhibitors and gentle treatment of the dog. Here are some specific areas to consider.

Corrections

You may not train or intensively practice with your dog anywhere on the show grounds, which includes the parking lot and the entire park, campus, or fairgrounds where the show is being held. "Grounds" in this case is a somewhat nebulous word and can lead to some strange interpretations. On one show circuit, some exhibitors were criticized by the AKC field representative for training on the grounds of the motel where most of the exhibitors were staying, several miles from the show site.

Otherwise, the intention of this part of the *Regulations* is quite clear. It was meant to stop people from setting up practice rings in the parking lot or on the other side of the show grounds and doing what was often perceived as abusive training where the public could observe the behavior. Many years ago, the AKC permitted actual practice rings on the grounds, but these were removed because of negative training (people were seen throwing dogs over jumps, or hitting or slapping their dogs). Exhibitors then tried to circumvent the prohibition against training on the grounds as described above.

There is disagreement among participants in obedience as to what constitutes abusive training. For those who train with inducive methods (praise, toys, and food rather than corrections), a jerk on a choke chain may be perceived as abusive. Other trainers might consider this a normal part of daily living with their dogs. In 1987, the AKC spelled out the rules for warming up dogs and training on the grounds in reasonably clear language. The memorandum published on the subject states: "A warm-up has the following characteristics:

1. It consists only of the activities contained in the Novice Heel on Lead exercise and a few (three or four) fronts and finishes *on lead* [italics mine].
2. It should be for a duration of less than five minutes.
3. It should be within approximately ten minutes of the time when the dog is going to enter the ring for judging.
4. It will not include any corrections. (In deciding what constitutes a correction, an individual must be guided by the same standard as would apply in the ring.)"

No other warm-up is permitted. I believe that this information has been helpful to clubs and exhibitors,

You may not train or intensively practice with your dog anywhere on the show grounds, which includes the parking lot and the entire park, campus, or fairgrounds where the show is being held.

The AKC defines warming up and training your dog on the showgrounds as follows:

1. Consists only of the activities in the Novice Heel on Lead exercise and a few fronts and finishes on lead.
2. Duration of less than five minutes.
3. Occurs within approximately ten minutes of the time when the dog is going to enter the ring for judging.
4. Will not include any corrections.

No other warm-up is permitted.

If your dog requires harsh correction in order to behave in the ring, perhaps you are showing him prematurely and need to spend more time training him.

because it provides reasonable guidelines and prevents a lot of slipping into bathrooms and behind parked cars for illicit activities at dog shows.

Your dog must be on leash at all times except when he is in the ring. Commands that you would normally use to walk your dog around the grounds (heel, down, etc.) are permitted. If your dog requires harsh correction in order to behave in the ring, perhaps you are showing him prematurely and need to spend some more time training him.

Controlling Your Dog

You are responsible for any damage done by your dog. It is your legal and ethical responsibility to prevent your dog from being a nuisance or a danger to other dogs and to their exhibitors.

Before you sign an entry form for an AKC show or obedience trial, read the agreement on the back. Among other things, it says that the exhibitor is responsible for any damage done by his or her dog. This means that you are liable for your dog's behavior. It is your legal and ethical responsibility to prevent your dog from being a nuisance or a danger to other dogs and to their exhibitors.

If you know that your dog has a tendency to look for trouble, don't show him until you are sure that he will not be the one to start a fight. It is bad enough when a dog that is normally peaceful becomes aggressive at a trial (generally in a response to the pressure of so many bodies in a limited area, or to the handler's tension), but to take a dog that you know you cannot control off leash into a show situation is inexcusable. If your dog attacks another dog, you must pull him off (speak to your instructor about ways to break up dog fights), and offer to assist the exhibitor of the other dog if veterinary attention is needed. You must accept financial responsibility for any injuries your dog causes to canines or to humans who are trying to separate combatant dogs.

*If your dog is expelled by the judge for attacking another dog in the ring three times, your dog will be **disqualified** and cannot be shown again at any AKC event unless you apply for and are granted reinstatement.*

If on three separate occasions your dog is expelled by the judge for attacking another dog in the ring, the AKC will notify you that the dog has been **disqualified** and cannot be shown again at any AKC event unless and until you apply for and are granted reinstatement. If you can prove to the AKC that there were extenuating circumstances, you may be given another chance. If not, that is the end of that dog's show career. If your dog attacks or attempts to attack a person even once (even if the person he attacks is his own handler), he will be disqualified immediately, and you will have to apply for reinstatement as described above.

Again, it is *absolutely inexcusable* for someone to take a known vicious dog to an obedience trial.

If your dog attacks or attempts to attack a person even once, he will be disqualified immediately.

Exercising Your Dog

This phrase has nothing to do with calisthenics; it refers to elimination of body wastes. It is important that your dog empty his bowels and bladder before he enters the ring. If he relieves himself at any time while in the ring for judging, he will not receive a qualifying score.

It is important that your dog empty his bowels and bladder before he enters the ring. If he relieves himself at any time while in the ring for judging, he will not receive a qualifying score.

The exception to this rule is if the dog leaves his mark, so to speak, during a run-off at the end of the class. Generally, the dog will simply lose the run-off. The rationale for this exception appears to be that the dog's score has already been entered in the judge's book and cannot be changed except to correct an arithmetic error. I have always considered this to be a philosophical contradiction. It seems to me that a dog that relieves himself while he is supposed to be working in the ring is hardly the epitome of obedience training and should not be rewarded with a qualifying score, much less a placement in a class; however, I have seen it happen on many occasions.

Some dogs have the frustrating habit of being unwilling to eliminate in a strange place. Try to find a surface similar to what he has at home, but respect any off-limits signs on the show or trial grounds. More and more show sites are being closed to dog shows because exhibitors are inconsiderate and permit their dogs to eliminate wherever they choose, ruining floors, lawns, etc.

Some dogs are unwilling to eliminate in a strange place. Try to find a surface similar to what he has at home, but respect any off-limits signs on the show or trial grounds.

Clubs must provide exercise areas for dogs. At indoor trials, these are generally covered with sawdust, and clean-up equipment is usually nearby. (At some larger all-breed shows, clean-up crews are hired to keep the grounds and pens clean.) If you must exercise your dog outside the designated area — or if he chooses to exercise himself — find the clean-up equipment or a member of the cleaning crew and see that the offending matter is removed immediately. Do not look the other way and pretend that it wasn't *your* dog that made the mess.

If your dog has not had a bowel movement before you take him into the ring, you may want to help nature along by inserting the business end of an unlit paper match into his rectum to stimulate some action. A baby suppository will have the same effect. After insertion, put the dog on a down-stay for five minutes, then take him out.

Enforcement

Behavior in the ring is handled by the judge. He or she can and will dismiss, excuse, or expel any handler who does not adhere to the spirit and letter of the Regulations.

Enforcement of the rules regarding sportsmanship rests in two areas. Behavior in the ring is handled by the judge. He or she can and will dismiss, excuse, or expel any handler who does not adhere to the spirit and letter of the *Regulations*. If an exhibitor willfully interferes with the performance of a competitor's dog, or if the judge suspects any cheating (such as carrying food in the ring, giving surreptitious corrections, having another person outside the ring signaling corrections to the dog, etc.), the judge will generally fail the dog. The dog can be shown the next day, hopefully in a more ethical fashion.

If a judge believes that a dog has been abused in the ring or on the trial grounds, or if the handler treats the judge in a discourteous manner, the judge will refer the matter to the Obedience Trial Committee of the show-giving club. This is known as "calling the Committee" on an exhibitor and is an unpleasant experience for all. A fellow exhibitor can also lodge a complaint.

If, however, a judge believes that a dog has been abused in the ring or on the trial grounds, or if the handler treats the judge in a discourteous manner (arguing about scores, maligning the judge's character, refusing to accept or throwing down a ribbon, standing at ringside making audible negative comments, etc.), the judge will refer the matter to the Obedience Trial Committee of the show-giving club. A fellow exhibitor can also lodge a complaint, especially if there were witnesses to the unsportsmanlike behavior. The committee will hold a hearing immediately (before the trial is over, if possible), and the exhibitor will have the opportunity to defend him or herself. The committee will make a decision on the spot. If the committee feels that the individual's behavior was prejudicial to the good of the sport, it will suspend the handler from exhibiting. This means that any dogs owned or co-owned by that exhibitor cannot be shown until the suspension is lifted, nor can the exhibitor handle a dog in the obedience or conformation ring or in the field or in herding events. The exhibitor can appeal the decision to the Board of Directors of the AKC, or may request reinstatement of privileges. The AKC, not the committee, determines the length of the suspension. It may run from one month to an indefinite period.

Be aware that there is a difference between having your *dog disqualified,* which only eliminates that particular dog from further competition, and having *yourself suspended,* which affects you and all dogs that you own or co-own.

Disqualification affects only one dog. Suspension affects all dogs that you own.

The Rep

The AKC maintains a staff of field representatives who attend larger shows all over the country. Some are now specializing in obedience trials and are extremely knowledgeable about the sport. Each of these individuals, known universally as "the rep," covers shows and trials in a particular geographic area. At a show or trial, the rep functions as a trained observer, a knowledgeable resource person, and a mediator. The rep does *not* make decisions about problems at a show; that is the job of the show or trial committee. The rep is a good source of information about rules and regulations, but the power of enforcement still rests with the trial committee.

Field representatives do not make decisions about problems at a show but are good sources of information about rules and regulations. The rep may discuss problems with the judge and/or file a written report with the AKC.

Final Considerations

Now that you have checked the catalogue, exercised your dog, and found your ring, there are a few more things to think about before you enter the ring.

If your class has started or is about to begin, take your entry ticket to the table at the ring entrance and ask for your armband (remember — the number assigned to you is on your entry ticket). Put the armband on your left arm, turned so that you can look down and see the number (upside down to you). This means that it will also be visible to the judge and other exhibitors. Don't hide the number in your armpit. It is not a secret.

Now, find a spot to settle yourself and your dog (if he is not crated somewhere else). Do not sit right next to the ring, because this may be distracting to a dog working in the ring. Furthermore, an occasional dog will decide that the spot his owner had chosen right next to

Before the Class Begins

1. Take your entry ticket to the table at the ring entrance and ask for your armband. Put the armband on your left arm, turned so that you can look down and see the number.
2. Find a spot to settle yourself and your dog.
3. Spend a few minutes watching what is going on in the ring.

Put your armband on your left arm, and be sure that the number is visible to you (upside down, of course).

Some judges employ unusual heeling patterns. Watching will help you move smoothly from exercise to exercise.

the ring is safe territory and will leave the ring if he becomes confused (or is feeling naughty) and head back to that spot. If there are rows of chairs, try to sit in the second row.

Spend a few minutes watching what is going on in the ring. Judges are required to standardize their heeling patterns as much as possible, meaning that you and your dog will follow the same pattern of turns, starts, and stops as the previous teams. You are likely to be nervous (to put it mildly), and it is helpful to have a mental picture of the pattern so that you will know which way to turn. Some judges employ unusual heeling patterns with unexpected twists, such as a halt in the ring entrance. Watching several dogs perform will help you move smoothly from exercise to exercise, because you will know where in the ring each one starts. If you are the first team in the ring, the judge may choose to describe the pattern to you. It is also permissible to ask, but the judge is not required to tell you.   ∎

In The Novice Ring

What To Expect from the Judge

It is the judge's responsibility to give you a courteous, thorough, unbiased, knowledgeable assessment of your dog's performance. He or she is also responsible for seeing that the ring conditions meet AKC specifications, especially regarding safe footing for dog and handler. This is more important in the advanced classes where the dog is required to jump. Some judges are warm and friendly; some are brisk and businesslike. You can obtain more information about what the AKC expects of its obedience judges from the booklet, *Guidelines to Obedience Judging,* available free upon written request. The judge has complete control of the ring. The judge's decisions are final and are not subject to discussion (see page 80). You, in turn, are expected to be courteous to the judge (at matches, too).

Handling Errors

Because obedience competition is an artificial situation — as opposed to, say, taking your dog for a walk in the park — there are rules governing how the exhibitor is expected to perform, in addition to those that apply to the dog. You and your dog are a team and must work together. Just as the dog will lose points or fail to qualify because he makes a mistake, the same fate awaits you if you err. The judge can and will fail the dog if the handler makes certain errors.

If your failure to qualify is not obvious, the judge will generally tell you about it before you leave the ring. The judge *must* inform every

It is the judge's responsibility to give you a courteous, thorough, unbiased, knowledgeable assessment of your dog's performance. The judge's decisions are final and are not subject to discussion. The judge must inform every exhibitor if his or her dog has qualified or not at the end of the group exercises and after the Directed Jumping in Utility.

exhibitor if his or her dog has qualified or not at the end of the group exercises and after the Directed Jumping in Utility.

Be aware that your dog may pass all of the individual exercises and still fail to qualify because he did not earn a total score of at least 170 points. This is known as "failing on points" and happens more often than you might imagine.

After I have described the handling requirements for each exercise, I will discuss proofing methods, as well as common handling errors and the criteria for passing or failing the exercise. This will help you to form an accurate image of a qualifying performance.

Non-Qualification Versus Disqualification

A non-qualifying score means that your dog failed to pass in one class at one show. However, a dog that is disqualified may not again compete at an AKC event unless and until the owner appeals to the AKC and is notified by the AKC that the dog has been reinstated.

Many exhibitors use these terms interchangeably; however, they have different meanings. A *non-qualifying* score (or NQ, flunk, bust, etc.) simply means that your dog failed to pass in one class at one show. You and the dog can go home, work on the problem exercise, and show again at the next trial. A disqualification, however, is a much more serious matter. A dog that is *disqualified* may not again compete at an AKC event unless and until the owner appeals the disqualification to the AKC and is notified by the AKC that the dog has been reinstated.

There are five reasons why a dog would be disqualified:

1. If it is blind.
2. If it is deaf.
3. If it has been artificially altered (see page 3).
4. If it attacks any person in the ring.
5. If it attacks another dog in the ring on three occasions.

Now that you know the difference, you can use the correct terminology and impress your fellow exhibitors with your expertise.

Being Excused from the Ring

Being excused from the ring means that you will not continue to perform any additional exercises, including the group exercises in both Novice and Open. Being excused applies only to the class involved and does not generally affect any other classes in which the dog is entered on that day or any other day. The exception to this rule is that a dog will be excused if he has stitches anywhere on his body and will not be allowed to compete again until the stitches have been removed.

If your dog is lame or ill or otherwise unfit to compete, the judge will excuse him. Before proceeding with any other class in which the dog may be entered, you must consider whether the condition is an isolated occurrence (the dog stepped on a burr that you have since removed and is now moving soundly) or if the condition is likely to continue (the dog has galloping diarrhea), and then decide if the dog needs to be taken to the veterinarian or otherwise removed from competition for one or more days.

There are a number of other reasons why a judge may excuse either the exhibitor or the dog (although you both must leave when this happens). If the dog, in the judge's opinion, is not under the handler's control (running madly around the ring as soon as the leash is taken off, barking continuously, urinating to mark territory, or even heeling so poorly on leash that the judge is certain that disaster will result when the lead is removed), the judge will excuse the dog. This is often done to protect other dogs from potential trouble.

I once judged an extremely pregnant woman with a huge dog that I had observed outside the ring lunging at other dogs and dragging the woman hither and yon. I continued to notice this behavior as the day wore on and hoped fervently that she would be exhibiting in a ring other than mine. No such luck. As their number was called, the woman got up and the dog dragged her to the gate of my ring in spite of several sharp collar corrections. The dog lifted his leg and urinated all over the ring entrance. I excused them before they ever entered the ring, because the dog was clearly not under the woman's

Being excused from the ring means that you will not continue to perform any additional exercises, including the group exercises in both Novice and open. Being excused applies only to the class involved and does not generally affect any other classes in which the dog is entered on that day or any other day.

If the dog, in the judge's opinion, is not under the handler's control, the judge will excuse the dog. This is often done to protect other dogs from potential trouble.

Exhibitors are most often excused for training in the ring, especially when they move toward the dog to correct him when he fails to jump or drop. Being excused is not a tragedy.

When the judge tells you that you are excused, respond pleasantly and promptly head out of the ring. Do not attempt to argue with the judge.

control and not ready to compete on that particular day.

Exhibitors are most often excused for training in the ring, especially when they move toward the dog to correct him when he fails to jump or drop. Being thus excused is not a major disaster and will not cause a black mark to be placed next to your name in the annals of the AKC. As a trainer and exhibitor, I sometimes feel that it is worth being excused to make a verbal correction in the ring. If I have been having a training problem with my dog, especially one that only seems to manifest itself in the ring, I will give a second command or even step toward my dog or toward the appropriate jump, once the dog has failed to respond to my first command. As long as there is nothing harsh about my command (and that includes calling the dog nasty names), and I do not touch the dog, no punitive measures should be taken by anyone. Making the correction on Saturday may result in a better performance on Sunday, or at least give me some satisfaction knowing that my dog has been forced to do the exercise. If the dog does not respond to a second or third command, call him to you and do not continue to press for a response. When the judge tells you that you are excused, respond pleasantly and promptly head out of the ring. Do not attempt to argue with the judge; he or she is merely exercising the responsibility to maintain full control of the ring and to comply with the *Regulations*.

Misbehavior

You are allowed to give only one command (or command and signal, if permitted) in most circumstances. *If you give a second command or signal (except on heeling) after an exercise has begun, you will fail the exercise.* If your dog is excited and refuses to sit at heel in spite of several commands from you, go ahead and *gently* position him with your hands, understanding that you will receive a substantial deduction (at least three points). This deduction will appear in the judge's book under the subtotal of your score, in a section marked "less penalty for misbehavior."

Other reasons for receiving a "below-the-line" deduction for misbehavior include:

● A dog barking between exercises.

- A dog running away from the handler between exercises (even if he comes back immediately).
- The handler making physical corrections with the hands or feet when positioning a dog before an exercise. If it is a question of losing a few points for *gently* positioning your dog with your hands versus being excused for having a dog that is not under control, the choice is clear. *Gently* does not mean smacking, hitting, kicking, or sharply jerking on the collar.

After the judge has said, "Exercise finished," many people will tell their dog to sit straight if their dog's position at the end of the exercise is not perfect. Not only do some judges consider this to be training in the ring and deduct points accordingly, but it is also of questionable value to telegraph to the judge that your dog sat crooked, because the judge may not have thought that was the case. Sour looks at the dog while he is heeling, sitting in front, or finishing can be equally detrimental to your score. This doesn't mean that you must maintain a poker face at all times. Keep your sense of humor about your dog's major goof-ups in the ring — or your own!

When the Dog Leaves the Ring

There is an old belief that a dog that leaves the ring will automatically fail. This is not stated anywhere in the *Regulations* and is not necessarily true. Under some circumstances, there could be no deduction for a dog leaving the ring, such as a dog that goes under a ring rope looking for a dumbbell in high grass. Even the dog that bolts from the ring may not lose a point.

Once, I was showing a dog that was afraid of men. Considering that the judge was male, the dog held himself together well, giving a creditable if not stunning performance — until I left him near the judge's table to stand next to the broad jump. A sudden gust of wind blew all of the papers off of the judge's table into the dog's face, and he was over the ring gates and across the park before I could open my mouth. The judge, considering this an unusual circumstance (and, I suspect, having trained a spooky dog himself), allowed me to collect my dog, calm him down, and repeat the exercise with no deduction. Other judges might have made a deduction but probably

There is an old belief that a dog that leaves the ring will automatically fail. This is not stated anywhere in the Regulations and is not necessarily true.

If the dog simply bolts from the ring but returns when called, some type of penalty should be assessed, and the judge may fail the dog.

would not have automatically failed the dog because of the papers blowing off of the table.

But what about the dog that simply bolts out of the ring to chase a squirrel, or because he sees something fascinating? If the handler is alert and calls the dog promptly, and the dog responds immediately, a stiff penalty should be assessed. However, no rule states that the dog must be failed. On the other hand, I would not fault a judge for failing a dog that behaved in this manner, because the dog is clearly, if temporarily, out of control.

Hands Off

Once you enter the Novice ring, you may not touch the dog except to pet him between exercises. You may not — under any circumstances — position him with your hands, knees, or feet.

Once you enter the Novice ring, you may not touch the dog except to pet him between exercises. You may guide the dog gently by the collar between exercises, but you may not — under any circumstances — position him with your hands, knees, or feet. If you teach your dog to pay attention on command ("watch me"), you may not touch the dog's head or muzzle when you tell him to look at you.

Rejudging

Ordinarily, your dog will have only one chance to perform each exercise. However, if unusual circumstances cause a dog to fail, the judge may allow the entire exercise to be repeated. This decision is strictly up to the judge. One of the most common occurrences requiring rejudging is the collapse of the ring enclosure during a Long Sit or Down exercise, or interference with one dog by another dog. If the unusual event only causes one or two dogs to fail, and the other dogs maintain their stays while exposed to the same distractions, the judge will probably *not* rejudge the failing dogs. This is why proofing is so important.

Entering the Ring

1. Empty your pockets of food treats, toys, jangling keys, and loose change.

Entering the Ring

When your number is called, you will enter the ring with your dog on a loose leash.

You may bend to give a signal at the dog's eye level only when the dog is in heel position.

1. Be sure to empty your pockets of any food treats and toys, and leave them at your seat or (if the judge does not object), on the table at the ring entrance. If you carry a set of noisy, jangling keys or five pounds of loose change in your pocket (men are the worst offenders), get rid of those items, too, before entering the ring. They can make enough noise to be considered an aid to the dog and are an annoyance to the judge. Also, spit out your gum.

2. Proceed to the spot where all of the other teams started, and have your dog sitting quietly in the heel position.

3. The judge will ask you if you are ready. It is permissible to call for the dog's attention before saying that you are (but remember not to touch him). It is a good idea to get in the habit of giving the same response every time the judge asks if you are ready (for example, replying, "Yes" or "Ready"). This is an extra, legal reminder to the dog that the action is about to start. Many handlers nod their heads in response, but a verbal response is clearer to the judge. Some handlers are so paralyzed with fear that they stand and let their eyes glaze over as a response to, "Are you ready?" This is rather frustrating to the judge and makes a poor impression.

2. Proceed to the spot where all of the other teams started, and have your dog sitting quietly in heel position.

3. The judge will ask if you are ready. Many handlers nod their heads, but a verbal response is clearer to the judge.

It is a good idea to use a cue word like "Ready" to let the dog know that the action is about to begin.

Your commands to the dog may be in any language, and you may substitute a hand signal for any command. You may not use the dog's name with a hand signal, except on exercises in which you are permitted to use the name, verbal command, and signal. When you do use both name and command, they must be spoken with no pause between them. Pausing between name and command is a handling error. Loud commands should also be penalized.

Commands

Your commands to the dog may be in any language, and you may substitute a hand signal for any command. You may not use the dog's name with a hand signal, except on exercises in which you are permitted to use the name, verbal command, and signal. You are not required to use the dog's name before a command. If your dog tends to anticipate commands, you may want to consider this option. When you do use both name and command, they must be spoken with no pause between them: "Fido, Sit." Not, "Fido . . . . . . Sit." *Pausing between name and command is a handling error.* Commands must be given in a normal tone of voice. Loud commands should be penalized.

Fouling the Ring

If your dog begins to urinate or have a bowel movement in the ring, attempt to move him off the mat, if any, then let him finish. The dog will fail to qualify but generally will be permitted to complete the exercises.

If your dog begins to urinate or have a bowel movement in the ring, attempt to move him off the mat, if any, then let him finish. Dragging the dog out of the ring merely extends the area of disaster. Be aware that the dog will fail to qualify but generally will be permitted to complete the exercises. The steward or clean-up crew will remove the debris.

If your dog assumes a position indicating that he is about to defecate, a good judge will stop you, ask you to leave the ring to let the dog finish his business, and then may or may not permit you to complete the exercise. If you see that your dog is showing his particular signs of having to go, you may ask the judge to allow you to leave the ring. While the judge will appreciate your thoughtfulness in not having to hold up the proceedings to have the ring cleaned, and not luring other dogs to the soiled spot in the ring, you will fail the class under either circumstance. This is why it is important to give your dog a chance to empty himself before entering the ring for any judging.

Individual Exercises

Heel on Leash and Figure 8

Footwork

The way in which you walk will affect your dog's performance and therefore your score on the heeling exercises. Heeling is an exercise in which the *dog* accompanies *you* — not the other way around.

Heeling is an exercise in which the dog accompanies you — not the other way around.

Pace. You set the pace for the team. Your pace should be brisk enough so that the dog must move at a trot. Walking too slowly can be considered as adapting your pace to that of the dog, resulting in points deducted for a handling error.

Your pace should be brisk enough so that the dog must move at a trot.

Consistency in Movement. You should also attempt to be consistent in all of your movements so that the dog will know what to expect. Your instructor will show you how to make good turns so that your footwork is an asset — not a liability — to your dog. If you train alone, consult one of the many books available or try to attend a training clinic in your area.

Be consistent in all of your movements so that the dog will know what to expect.

Walking in a Straight Line. You must also practice walking in a straight line. This is easier to do when walking on mats. Be sure to keep the dog on the mat, while you walk on the slippery floor in your non-skid shoes. If your dog is heeling wide (too far to your left), you must not move to the left to make him look better. *This is a handling error and will result in points being lost.* Similarly, do not move to the right to avoid a dog that is crowding you. Once you are in the ring, it is too late to correct these errors. *Let the dog make the mistakes!* Your attempts to compensate will be noticed by most judges, and they will be unimpressed by your tactics. In most cases, not only will there be a deduction for the dog's error, but also a deduction for the handling error made in an attempt to conceal the dog's mistake.

Practice walking in a straight line. Do not attempt to cover up your dog's mistakes by stepping to the right or left.

Small and Short-Legged Dogs. People with small or short-legged dogs must be especially conscious of their

Correct heel position from the front.

Correct heel position from the side.

footwork. It is important that they refrain from letting their feet drift in front of the dog and that they do not kick up their heels in the dog's face when doing the fast, because this will cause the dog to lag or to swing wide.

Change of Pace. When the judge calls for a slow pace, you must make a noticeable change in your speed. Most trainers advise long, slow, even steps, rather than tiny, mincing ones. When the fast is called, you must run. It is *not* true that your dog must break into a gallop, as long as he stays in "heel" position. If your dog bounces up and down with excitement when you speed up and his feet actually leave the ground, the judge should make a deduction. You are permitted to take several steps to change from one pace to another and back again. Abrupt changes of pace make for a jerky-looking heeling performance.

Halting. Similarly, you may take two or three steps to halt after the command is given (but not five or six steps). You must stop in a straight line, without stepping to your right or left to make the dog's sit appear straighter. Once you have stopped, do not shuffle your feet forward or backward. If your dog fails to sit, do not correct him verbally or physically. He will lose several points but will not fail the exercise. If your dog swings around and sits in front of you, or goes all the way around you, wait until the judge again says, "Forward," and then gently guide the dog into heel position with the leash and walk on.

Turns. When making left and right turns, do not round the corners. Make a square turn, without pausing, but not in military fashion. Do not pause on the about turns, because this will be considered an illegal aid to the dog. Also, be careful not to back into the about turns, because this is another way of accommodating the dog.

Have your instructor or a friend observe your footwork with these factors in mind. It is easy to get into bad habits while training — habits that will cost unnecessary deductions from your score. If you train alone, there are a number of training books that teach good footwork.

If you have a small dog, refrain from letting your feet drift in front of the dog and from kicking your heels in the dog's face when doing the fast.

When the fast is called, you must run. It is not *true that your dog must break into a gallop, as long as he stays in heel position.*

You may take two or three steps to halt after the command is given. Stop in a straight line. Do not shuffle your feet forward or backward. If your dog fails to sit, do not correct him verbally or physically.

When making left and right turns, make a square turn without pausing. Do not pause on the about turns or back into the about turns. Be sure that you turn in place, rather than walking in an arc (a "U" turn).

A final word on footwork: While it is helpful to the dog when the handler moves in a consistent manner, the AKC does not require any specific footwork. You will not lose points for starting to walk with the right foot, although handlers are traditionally taught to start with the left foot. Inexperienced match judges are notorious for mistakenly deducting points for this.

Straightening Your Dog

If your dog is not sitting straight when the judge asks if you are ready to begin the heeling pattern, you may tell him to straighten himself. Don't make endless circles to straighten the dog.

If your dog is not sitting straight when the judge asks if you are ready to begin the heeling pattern, you may tell him to straighten himself. Many handlers become obsessed with this initial step and circle around and around attempting to get the dog into the desired position. This is time consuming and annoying to the judge, who has a limited amount of time allotted to judge each dog. If the exhibitor repeats this action enough times, the judge may begin to deduct points for the dog's lack of response to command.

If it is consistent with your training program, it may be advisable to teach your dog to straighten himself on command without any circling. Under any circumstances, if the dog does not respond after one or two commands, forget about it and tell the judge that you are ready. Remember — judging does not begin until you say that you are ready, except when the dog is obviously refusing to respond to commands.

Hand Position for the Heel on Leash

The leash may be held in either hand or in both hands. There should be enough slack in the leash to show that the dog is maintaining heel position of his own free will, but the leash should not hang down so that the dog is likely to trip over it.

The leash may be held in either hand or in both hands. There should be enough slack in the leash to show that the dog is maintaining heel position of his own free will, will, but the leash should not hang down so that the dog is likely to trip over it. If the dog lags or forges, do not let out more of the leash in the hope that the judge will not notice that the dog is not in heel position. Again, let the dog make the mistake, if any.

Do not change hand position during the course of the heeling exercise.

Your hand position should be comfortable for you and should look natural. A good rule of thumb is, would this be a likely hand position for a person walking a well-mannered dog along the street? If not, you may be penalized for a handling error.

Whatever hand position you choose, do not change it during the course of the heeling exercise. Exhibitors lose many points by moving their hands during the heeling exercise, especially on the halts. In some cases, this is a result of poor training. The dog has learned to wait for a slight tightening of the leash as a signal to sit, instead of sitting because the handler has stopped walking. It can also be a function of nervousness. Take pains to avoid these movements, whatever the cause. If you are not sure if you are telegraphing subtle correction to the dog with the leash, have somebody observe you. Hand position becomes more critical in the Heel Free, as we will see.

Facial Expression

Do not stare at your dog while you are heeling. This can be counted as a handling error and can also make the dog lag, because he is anticipating a correction. You may watch the dog out of the corner of your eye. Remember — if he is not in heel position, it is too late to do anything about it once you are in the ring. Try to maintain a pleasant facial expression rather than glaring at the dog. This is supposed to be *fun,* after all.

Do not stare at your dog while you are heeling. This can be counted as a handling error and can also make the dog lag.

Do not turn and try to stare your dog into heel position. Not only is it a handling error, but it generally makes dogs lag farther behind to avoid those intimidating eyes.

You must not anticipate turns or changes of pace. Wait for the judge to give the order.

Anticipating Turns or Pace Changes

You *must not* anticipate turns or changes of pace. Wait for the judge to give the order. It is easy to anticipate commands, especially if the ring is small or the judge is slow to give commands. If the judge runs you into a wall or ring barrier, stop and wait for further instructions. Some judges have problems with depth perception and have difficulty giving the turn commands at the proper time. It is also possible, I assure you, to become so fascinated watching a dog's performance (either because he is very good or very bad) that a judge may simply forget to give the turn command. When I do this, I do not penalize the exhibitor but usually apologize, back the team up several steps, and start again. Many instructors have their trainees practice sits directly in front of a wall or barrier as preparation for such an occurrence.

Proofing Heeling

The best proofing for consistently good heeling is to teach your dog to pay attention to you at all times.

Teaching Your Dog to Pay Attention. The best proofing that I can suggest for consistently good heeling is to teach your dog to pay attention to you at all times. A dog that is intently concentrating on his handler is unlikely to notice distracting elements in or around the ring. This kind of attention is beautiful to observe. Some trainers appear to have velcroed their dogs into heel position, and the dogs never vary an inch from the desired spot. In the real world where most of us train and exhibit, however, many potential disasters can lure a dog out of heel position.

Practice heeling, fronts, and finishes and work on dog attention in front of the local supermarket — dodging carts, children, and pneumatic doors. I never train in my backyard, because I believe that the dogs get far too comfortable there.

Setting Up Potential Situations. To proof a dog against being lured, you must set up these potential situations in training or at fun matches and work with your dog until he will ignore them (at least most of the time). I often practice heeling, fronts, and finishes and work on dog attention in front of the local supermarket — dodging carts, children, and pneumatic doors. If you live in a rural area, you may have to travel to a nearby town for some worthwhile opportunities to proof against distractions. I lug dogs and equipment to a different place every time I train and frequently drive 120 miles to attend classes in different locations. I never train in my backyard, because I believe that the dogs get far too comfortable there and do not learn to perform under difficult conditions.

Common Distractions. The more common distractions center around food and the presence of unfamiliar dogs. Spectators, or inconsiderate exhibitors, will set out wonderful picnics within six inches of the ring barrier or sometimes will lean over the ring barrier and drop food right onto the heeling area. Train your dog to heel past, around, and over different types of food, making whatever corrections are necessary to keep his attention on you.

Some dogs do not like to get their feet wet or dirty and are especially unwilling to step or sit where another dog has eliminated. The Keeshond (pictured holding the dumbbell in the Open section) was exceptionally good at maintaining heel position about ten inches off of the ground if there was a wet spot in our path.

Other potential distractions to be dealt with in training include:

- Children running at large or crying.
- Family members.
- Dogs of the same breed.
- Different types of terrain (tall grass, mud, or sprinkler heads).

You will often be heeling along a ring barrier while a dog on the other side is working. Be sure that your dog will not stop to watch, to visit, or to fight. Some dogs refuse to heel along blank walls, so be sure that your dog has had this experience before entering a show.

Dogs That Are Afraid of People. If you have a dog that is afraid of people, have a pretend judge follow you closely as you heel in practice, giving loud commands and occasionally deliberately getting in the way. Even dogs that are not shy can be unnerved by strange-looking or strange-acting judges. At one show, both the dog and I were astonished to find the judge running alongside us, only a foot away, as we did the fast. This unexpected behavior affected both of our performances.

Distractions to Proof Against

- *Food.*
- *Children running at large or crying.*
- *Family members.*
- *Dogs of the same breed.*
- *Bitches in season.*
- *Different types of terrain (tall grass, mud, or sprinkler heads).*
- *Activities in the next ring.*

If you have a dog that is afraid of people, have a pretend judge follow you closely as you heel in practice, giving loud commands and occasionally deliberately getting in the way.

Practice unusual heeling patterns. Be sure that your dog will do about turns in the ring gate and halts against the ring barrier.

Practicing Unusual Heeling Patterns. It is a good idea to practice unusual heeling patterns. Be sure that your dog will do about turns in the ring gate and halts against the ring barrier. Judges are no longer permitted to give halts while the dog is moving at a slow or fast pace, but many trainers practice them anyway to sharpen the dog's sits (or in case the judge forgets).

The Figure 8

After you have praised the dog for completing the heeling pattern:

Tips for the Figure 8

- *Start in either direction. Unless your dog crowds badly, you may want to start to your left. Starting to the right often encourages the dog to lag.*
- *The dog must change pace as the handler moves around the posts: faster on the outside and slower on the inside. Maintain a steady, brisk pace so that the dog adapts to you, not you to him.*
- *Keep your circles around the posts even.*
- *Stand up straight.*

1. Move to the spot where the Figure 8 will take place.
2. Face the judge, standing squarely equidistant from the two posts, and two to three feet back from them if there is adequate space.
3. You may start in either direction. Unless your dog crowds badly, you may want to start to your left. Starting to the right often encourages the dog to lag. Check with your instructor.
4. In the Figure 8, *the dog must change pace* as the handler moves around the posts: faster on the outside and slower on the inside. It is important that you maintain a steady, brisk pace so that the dog adapts to you — not you to him.
5. Keep your circles around the posts even. Do not make a wide circle when the dog is on the inside to avoid being crowded. If your dog lags when he is on the outside circle, do not let the leash out, hoping that the judge will not notice that the dog is out of heel position. The judge will not be fooled.
6. Try to stand up straight while doing the Figure 8, keeping your shoulders level as you circle.
7. When the Figure 8 is completed, surrender your lead to the steward and move to the spot where the Stand for Examination will take place.

Remember — from now on you may gently guide the dog — by the collar only — between exercises. Some trainers advise their students to try to avoid guiding the dog physically at all, but rather to rely on voice control. Other trainers suggest that rather than holding the live ring of a slip collar to guide the dog, you put your hand on the chain or fabric of the collar to avoid any hint of correction.

Proofing the Figure 8

Accustom your dog to all types of people who might serve as posts for the Figure 8: tall, short, and fat, people of different races, and people wearing rain gear or large sun hats. Have the people helping you cough loudly or glare at the dog while serving as posts. Otherwise, the proofing is similar to that outlined for heeling on lead, with one addition.

As a judge, I have often seen dogs sniff the people acting as posts as though they had bathed in liver. In my classes, we have the "post" people put pieces of smelly food on their shoes as the dog is heeling by, or actually try to tempt the dog out of heel position with a treat or a toy. This proofing prevents post sniffing.

Common Handling Errors

Common handling errors for the Heel on Leash and Figure 8 are:

- Walking too slowly, adapting your pace to that of the dog.
- Moving to the left if your dog is heeling wide, or moving to the right to avoid a dog that is crowding you.
- Circling around and around, attempting to get the dog into the desired position.
- Having an incorrect hand position, or moving hands during the exercise.
- Staring at your dog while heeling.
- Keeping the leash tight so that the dog is forced to stay in position.
- Giving extra verbal commands to the dog.
- Continuously jerking on the leash.

Pass or Fail?

It is difficult to fail the Heel on Leash, but some dogs manage. Behaviors that would cause the dog to fail include:

- Never being in heel position (either lagging behind or forging ahead).

Accustom your dog to all types of people who might serve as posts for the Figure 8: tall, short, and fat, people of different races, and people wearing rain gear or large sun hats. Have the people helping you cough loudly or glare at the dog while serving as posts.

Common Handling Errors

- *Walking too slowly.*
- *Moving to the left if your dog is heeling wide, or moving to the right to avoid a dog that is crowding you.*
- *Circling around and around, attempting to get the dog into the desired position.*
- *Having an incorrect hand position, or moving hands during the exercise.*
- *Staring at your dog while heeling.*
- *Keeping the leash so tight that the dog is forced to stay in position.*
- *Giving extra verbal commands to the dog.*
- *Continuously jerking on the leash.*

Fail

- *Never being in "heel" position.*
- *Attempting to leave the ring.*
- *Stopping completely.*

Stand for Examination is the only exercise in the Novice class in which you may physically manipulate your dog. It is courteous to stand the dog facing the judge. Stand your dog squarely.

Stand for Examination Procedure

1. *Stand up straight with both hands off of the dog and his collar.*
2. *Give the "stay" command and walk directly forward until you are six feet from your dog.*
3. *Turn and face the dog and stand quietly.*
4. *On the judge's order, return around the dog to your right and stop in heel position.*

- Attempting to leave the ring.
- Stopping completely.
- Failing to sit at heel at any time (this varies from judge to judge).

Stand for Examination

Positioning Your Dog

This is the only exercise in the Novice class in which you may physically manipulate your dog. It is courteous to stand the dog facing the judge. Some shy dogs, however, are less apt to break if approached by the judge from one side or the other. If you have a shy dog, experiment to see if this is applicable. If so, position your dog accordingly in the ring. (There is no guarantee, of course, that the judge will not move around to examine the dog squarely from the front.)

You may take any reasonable amount of time to position the dog. Stand your dog squarely rather than in an exaggerated show pose to lessen the chances of his moving to a more comfortable position after you leave.

Once the dog is standing comfortably:

1. Stand up straight and be sure that both hands are off of the dog and his collar. I often tell my more nervous students to count their hands before giving the "stay" command to be sure that both hands are off of the dog.
2. Give the "stay" command and walk directly forward until you are six feet from your dog. Generally, this distance is equal to three normal steps or two large steps.
3. Turn and face the dog and stand quietly until the examination is complete.
4. On the judge's order, return around the dog to your right, and be careful to stop in heel position.
5. The dog does not have to sit after this exercise but can be freed and praised directly from the standing position, depending on the training method used.

Proofing the Stand

Technically, judges are only supposed to touch the dog on the head, body (usually the back), and rump. However, many judges run their hands from forehead to

Make sure that BOTH hands are off the dog before giving the "stay" signal. Holding the collar like this will cost substantial points, or could cause you to fail for giving an extra "stay" command.

tail, and some even press on the dog's back or rump. Prepare your dog for these eventualities.

Large Breeds or Aggressive Dogs. If you have a large breed, or one with a reputation for aggressiveness, you will find some anxious judges who make no contact with the dog's body at all, passing their hands two inches above the dog. Or, they may touch the dog so lightly as to tickle him. They may approach the dog fearfully and hesitantly, which tends to upset many dogs. Again, be sure that your dog will not be disturbed by any of these odd examinations.

Many judges run their hands from forehead to tail and even press on the dog's back or rump. Prepare your dog for these eventualities. Some judges are fearful about handling a large or possibly aggressive dog and will not touch the dog. Be sure that your dog will not be disturbed by these odd examinations.

Judges go to great lengths to avoid distressing the little fellows. Some will get down on their knees to perform the exam. Make sure that your little dog will not be frightened or take it as an invitation to jump in the judge's lap and get in a few friendly kisses.

Smaller Dogs. The dogs that suffer the worst abuses on this exercise (and therefore need the most proofing) are the smaller dogs, particularly the toy breeds. Judges appear to be afraid that these dogs will break when they are touched and go to great lengths to avoid distressing the little fellows. Some will get down on their knees to perform the exam. While this is an error on the judge's part, make sure that your little dog will not be frightened by it or take it as an invitation to jump in the judge's lap and get in a few friendly kisses.

Clipboards, Ties, and Scarves. All dogs should be exposed to having a clipboard waved around their heads and having a tie or scarf fall on them during the examination.

Prepare your dog for any occurrence on the Stand for Examination. While this dog did not enjoy posing with a scarf in her face and a clipboard menacing her head, she has been proofed to tolerate just about anything.

Common Handling Errors

The most common handling errors for the Stand for Examination are:

- Holding the dog's head or collar in one hand while giving the stay command and signal.
- Backing away from the dog.
- Going farther than six feet away.
- Not returning all the way to heel position.

Pass or Fail?

If the dog remained standing where he was left until the examination was completed, he should pass, although he will lose points for moving his feet. A dog that moves away from the place where he was left before or during the exam will not pass. This is a matter of interpretation, but it would be safe to assume that a dog moving one body length from his original position would fail. Judges differ in their opinions.

Similarly, judges differ in their interpretations of shyness. The regulations state that a dog that "displays shyness" should receive a score of zero, but does this refer to a dog that leans away from the judge, without ever moving its feet, or to one that moves one foot or two feet? Most judges will not penalize a dog that basically stands his ground. A dog that growls or snaps, however, should always fail. If your dog walks away or sits or lies down after the examination, he will lose points but should not fail the exercise.

Heel Free

Generally, the Heel Free will follow the same pattern as the Heel on Leash, and the same rules apply.

Hand Position

The position of the handler's hands on this exercise has been a matter of some controversy. In the most recent revision of the *Regulations,* the acceptable positions are spelled out clearly. Your hands may be in one of two positions on the Heel Free. They may move naturally at your sides, rising slightly for balance during the fast, or the left hand may be held at the waist while the right

Common Handling Errors

- *Holding the dog's head or collar in one hand while giving the "stay" command and signal.*
- *Backing away from the dog.*
- *Going farther than six feet away.*
- *Not returning all the way to heel position.*

Pass

- *If the dog remained standing where he was left until the examination was completed.*

Fail

- *If a dog moves away from the place where he was left before or during the exam.*
- *If a dog growls or snaps.*

This dog is heeling in perfect position. The handler's left hand is raised to waist level and held against the body.

Your hands may move naturally at your sides, rising slightly for balance during the fast, or the left hand may be held at the waist while the right hand moves naturally. Failing to hold your hands in one of these positions for the Heel Free will result in a substantial deduction from your score.

hand moves naturally. Let's examine these two options.

If you have a dog whose head does not come above your knee, the first option is probably the best, because holding your hand up out of the way for a ten-inch dog looks rather silly. Both hands must move as you walk. You may not hold your left hand rigidly at your side. If you choose the second option, be certain that your left hand and arm are in place before you tell the judge that you are ready to begin the heeling exercise. Your hand must be centered at the approximate place that you would wear a belt buckle, and your arm must be against your body, not winging out at the elbow. Your hand may be flat against your body, or you may make a fist. Just be sure that your hand touches your waist at all times. Failing to hold your hands in one of these positions will result in a substantial deduction from your score.

If Your Dog Leaves Heel Position

If your dog stops or leaves heel position, or starts to bolt out of the ring, do not wait for the judge's order. Immediately give a firm command to heel (and a signal as well), and move on. If the dog responds, he will lose some points but may still qualify. Be alert for this and act promptly if it occurs.

If your dog stops or leaves heel position, or starts to bolt out of the ring, immediately give a firm command to heel and move on.

Proofing the Heel Free

The same problems occur on this exercise as on the Heel on Leash, and the proofing is therefore the same. The one difference is the dog that knows he is free and tends to bolt as soon as the exercise begins, or after the first about turn. This may occur for a number of reasons. The dog may lack confidence or may have learned to dislike heeling to such an extent that he exits at the first opportunity. These are training problems to be discussed with your instructor.

In some cases, however, I believe that the handler causes the problem by moving in such a way that the dog becomes confused and is unsure of what to do. Generally, handlers move much more slowly when the dog is off-lead, or change their body posture to stare at the dog because they do not trust him to stay in position. The more oddly the handler behaves, the more uncertain the dog becomes, initiating a self-perpetuating cycle. Once the lead is off, move with the same or even greater speed and confidence than you did earlier, even if you don't really believe that the dog will do well. "Act as if" and you may see dramatic improvements.

The same problems occur on the Heel Free as on the Heel on Leash, and the proofing is therefore the same. The one difference is the dog that knows he is free and tends to bolt as soon as the exercise begins, or after the first about turn. These are training problems. In some cases, however, I believe that the handler causes the problem by moving in such a way that the dog becomes confused and is unsure of what to do.

Common Handling Errors

The most common handling errors for the Heel Free are:

- Failing to hold your hands in the correct position.
- Moving in such a way that the dog becomes confused and is unsure of what to do.
- See the common handling errors listed under the Heel on Leash.

Common Handling Errors

- *Failing to hold your hands in the correct position.*
- *Moving in such a way that the dog becomes confused.*
- *See the common handling errors listed under the Heel on Leash.*

Pass

- *If a dog stays in heel position through at least 50 percent of the pattern.*

Fail

- *If a dog receives more than one extra command.*

The Recall Procedure

1. Your dog should be seated squarely.
2. When the judge orders you to leave, give your command and/or signal to "stay," and walk briskly away from your dog.
3. Turn and face your dog squarely. Allow enough room for him to finish and set your feet in the position that you will maintain until the exercise is complete.
4. Your hands must hang naturally at your sides.
5. When you call the dog, use a pleasant tone of voice and smile.
6. Do not make obvious head movements while following the dog's progress as he approaches you.
(Continued on next page)

Pass or Fail?

The Heel Free is probably the one exercise in which this determination is most difficult to predict. The exact same performance may cause a dog to fail one day and pass the next. I can only offer you my own criteria as a judge. I will pass a dog that stays in heel position through at least 50 percent of the pattern. In almost every case, a dog receiving more than one extra command will fail.

The Recall

The Exercise

Following the Heel Free, move to the position where the Recall is to begin.

1. See that your dog is seated squarely on the mat, if any.
2. When the judge orders you to leave, give your command and/or signal to "stay," and walk briskly away from your dog. Do not creep away, sneaking looks at him over your shoulder. Act as though you believe that he is going to wait for your recall command.
3. Turn and face your dog squarely, being careful to allow enough room for him to finish, and *set your feet in the position that you will maintain until the exercise is complete.* Moving your feet after you have called the dog should be considered a handling error. If you move them after the dog has sat in front of you, you will certainly receive a hefty deduction for adapting to the dog. If you are working on mats, be sure to stand either on the front or back edge of the cross mat (see photo). If you stand a foot or so behind the front edge of the cross mat, your dog may stop where the mats meet, especially if there is a piece of tape across the juncture, and may wind up sitting too far away from you.
4. *Your hands must hang naturally at your sides.*
5. When you call the dog, use a pleasant tone of voice and smile (you're almost through).
6. Do not make obvious head movements while following the dog's progress as he approaches you. Stand

Think about where you can best position yourself for the Recall. This little dog is reluctant to cross the tape and has sat out of reach. Had the handler stood with her toes on the tape, the dog would have qualified. Big dogs also stop at mat crossings or strips of tape.

Stand up straight and look pleasant when calling your dog.

If the dog does not sit straight in front, do not sway your body to create the illusion of a good front. As you can see, you have only compounded the dog's error with your own.

7. *If the dog does not sit in front, do nothing.*
8. *If the dog passes you by and heads out of the ring, call him back.*
9. *If your dog fails to come on your command, wait several seconds. You may then choose to give him a second · command.*

The dog may finish to the right or to the left.

up straight, and do not sway to one side or the other to make the front appear perfect if it is off-center.

7. If the dog does not sit in front, and either stands or proceeds directly to heel position, do nothing.
8. If the dog passes you by and heads out of the ring, call him back before he reaches the exit.
9. If your dog fails to come on your command, wait several seconds to see if he is merely reacting slowly. You may then choose to give him a second command. He has already failed the exercise but should not be allowed to ignore your command. Frequently, the judge will order you to give the second command.

The Finish

The finish is not a principal part of any exercise. It can be a source of many lost points, however. The dog may finish to the right or the left. Many exhibitors prefer

The handler stands still while the dog finishes.

to teach their dogs to finish in both directions. Then, if the dog sits too far to one side on the sit in front, they can send him to heel position more smoothly.

Dogs must move smartly to the heel position, but there is no requirement that the dog jump in the air while finishing. The jump or flip finish is very impressive to watch, and often is fun for the dog, but also provides an extra opportunity for the dog to bump or touch the handler, thereby receiving a deduction.

The dog will lose points if he stops to gaze at the spectators or to sniff, or oozes himself slowly into the final sit. Handlers are again prone to attempt to assist the dog — usually unconsciously — by moving their heads, shoulders, or knees.

1. Give either a signal or a command to finish, not both. Do not move your feet.
2. Do not follow your dog's progress after giving him the command or signal to finish, but watch out of the corner of your eye for him to appear in heel position.
3. If the dog does not respond to the finish command, wait for the judge to say, "Exercise finished," then release your dog.

Tips for the Finish

- *Do not follow your dog's progress after giving him the signal or command to finish, but watch out of the corner of your eye for him to appear in heel position.*
- *If the dog does not respond to the finish command, wait for the judge to say, "Exercise finished," then release your dog.*

(Continued on next page)

• *If the dog anticipates the finish, with or without stopping to sit in front, the judge should give you an additional command to finish. Give your dog the finish command.*

4. If the dog anticipates the finish, with or without stopping to sit in front, the judge should give you an additional command to finish. Give your dog the finish command or signal.
5. If the dog moves, or adjusts himself, he will get some credit for the finish. If you do not give the command or the dog fails to respond in some way, you will be hit with two substantial deductions, one for the anticipation and a second for the failure to finish.

Proofing the Recall and Finish

Anticipation. The problem that most often requires proofing is anticipation, or having the dog come when the handler calls his name, rather than waiting for the actual command to come. There are two ways to approach this problem.

To proof against anticipation, either drop the name when calling the dog or teach the dog to move only on the come command.

If the dog comes on his name, either drop the name and use just the command, or practice making the dog wait for the actual command word. Say the dog's name, followed by "wait" or "stay," and make an appropriate correction if the dog moves forward. Sometimes the dog will anticipate because of subtle body English signals given by the handler. Practice making the dog wait while you take a deep breath, twitch your hands, or flex your knees, or have someone else call a command similar to yours.

Distractability is handled the same as in the heeling exercise: having the dog do recalls over food and around obstacles. If your dog is likely to bolt, practice near an open door.

Distractability. Distractability is handled the same as in the heeling exercise: having the dog do recalls over food and around obstacles. Be sure that your dog will come straight in past a line of people and dogs (spectators and other exhibitors sitting at ringside) without swinging wide to avoid them or stopping to visit.

Common Handling Errors

• *Using body motions when calling the dog.*
• *Not standing with the arms hanging naturally at the sides any time the dog is coming toward the handler.*

Common Handling Errors

Handlers commonly lose points on the Recall for:

• Using body motions when calling the dog (bending from the neck or the waist or extending the arms; bending the knees while calling the dog).
• *Not* standing with the arms hanging naturally at the sides any time the dog is coming toward the handler.

Handler error! The handler is bending from the waist and flailing his arms about — all deductible movements.

A perfect sit in front.

Here, the handler makes a handling error by bending back to watch the dog's progress.

- *Screaming commands to the dog.*
- *Assisting the dog's finish.*
- *Moving your feet after calling the dog.*

Pass

- *If the dog waited to be called without moving forward.*
- *If the dog came on the first command.*
- *If the dog stopped within an arm's reach.*

Fail

- *If the dog comes in and sits out of reach.*
- *If the dog got up and made any movement toward you before you called him.*

- Screaming commands to the dog.
- Assisting the dog's finish with body English.
- Moving your feet after calling the dog.

Pass or Fail?

If the dog waited to be called without moving forward, came on the first command, and stopped within an arm's reach, he probably passed. If he stood or lay down before he was called, points will be deducted. If he got up and made any movement toward you before you called him, he probably failed.

Points can also be lost if the dog does not come directly to you, stops to sniff or look around, or comes in slowly.

The dog that comes in and sits out of reach will also fail. This is a judgment call. According to the *Regulations,* a dog is in reach if he is close enough so that the handler could touch the dog's head without stretching. This is somewhat misleading: if a six-foot-tall man is showing a dachshund, there is no way that he could touch the dog's head without stretching. Several years ago a different and somewhat more reasonable criterion appeared in the AKC's *Guidelines for Obedience Judges.* It said that a dog was considered out of reach if an average

You may not pick up or carry your dog at any time in the obedience ring.

person could walk between dog and handler without touching either. While this criterion no longer appears in the *Guidelines,* it remains a good rule of thumb.

When the Recall Is Completed
When the Recall exercise is completed:

1. Praise your dog and walk toward the ring entrance with the dog under control.
2. Take the leash from the steward or off the table and attach it before you leave the ring.
3. Never pick up your dog until you are out of the ring, or you will lose points under "Misbehavior."
4. It is courteous to thank the judge for his or her time.
5. Be sure that your attitude is positive, even if the dog failed miserably. The dog does not know that your experience in the ring was negative, but if you telegraph your displeasure to him, you may shake his

When the Recall is completed, praise your dog but never pick up your dog until you are out of the ring. Thank the judge for his or her time. Keep a positive attitude, even if your dog failed miserably.

confidence and affect future performances. If you feel that you cannot control your temper (and some very bright dogs appear to delight in testing their handlers by acting totally untrained in the ring), arrange to have a friend take the dog from you as you leave the ring, and keep the dog isolated until you have cooled down.

Group Exercises

The judge will usually advise the stewards as to how many dogs he or she will judge before breaking for a set of group exercises. If twelve or fewer dogs are entered in the class, there will be only one set of stays.

It is important that you keep track of when the break will occur. You would be wise to see that your dog has been exercised and given a drink by the time the last dog in the group is in the ring for the individual exercises. Be sure that your dog is awake and alert as you listen for the stewards to call the dogs in your group to line up in catalogue order. Be courteous enough to be available when this happens; don't be the person who has to be called and called, holding up the entire class.

Remember — unless your dog has been excused, expelled, or disqualified, he must do the group exercises even if he has non-qualified on the individual exercises. If you have a time conflict with another ring and your dog has already failed, you may ask the judge to excuse you from the group exercises. This is the judge's option, so if he or she does not agree to excuse you, you must appear.

Before group exercises on a hot day at an outdoor show, you may want to wet your dog down to keep him comfortable. Be sure to wet his head, chest, and groin thoroughly, as these areas will affect his comfort the most.

When you enter the ring with the other dogs:

1. Pay attention to the spot where you place your dog. If it is an outdoor trial, look for a flat surface with

Unless your dog has been excused, expelled, or disqualified, he must do the group exercises even if he has non-qualified on the individual exercises.

Procedures for Group Exercises

1. *Pay attention to the spot where you place your dog. If it is an outdoor trial, look for a flat surface with no burrs, twigs, etc. At an indoor show, do not place the dog where two mats are taped together, or where a dog previously fouled the ring.*

(Continued on next page)

no burrs, twigs, anthills, etc. At an indoor show, try to avoid placing the dog where two mats are taped together, or where a dog previously fouled the ring. You usually have the leeway to move your dog a few inches to one side of a potential problem area.

2. Remove your armband and leash. Turn to your left (toward the dog) and place them on the ground, several feet behind the dog. Should your dog get up when you turn, you will be between your dog and the next dog in line, so that he is less likely to come nose-to-nose with his neighbor.

3. If there is a dog in your group that has broken position and started fights at local matches or previous shows, you may *not* ask to change your order or to be in a different group to avoid the problem dog. You should inform the steward and/or the judge, in a calm and honest manner, of your concern. No judge wants a dog fight in the ring. The judge will be sure to keep a close eye on the likely offender.

2. Remove your armband and leash. Turn to your left (toward the dog) and place them on the ground, several feet behind the dog.

3. If there is a dog in your group that has started fights, you may not ask to change your order. Inform the steward and/or the judge of your concern.

When placing your leash and armband behind the dog before the Long Sit, turn INTO the dog to prevent his moving with you to confront the next dog, as illustrated below. This could be the start of a dog fight.

Some people avoid eye contact with the dog. Others maintain constant eye contact. Either way, you may not attempt to control your dog through any obvious facial contortions or body movements.

The Long Sit

Eye Contact/Body Movement

During this exercise, some people go to great lengths to avoid eye contact with their dog, even to the point of appearing a bit odd as they gaze off into space. Others maintain constant eye contact with the dog. Check with your instructor. Either way, you may not attempt to control your dog through any obvious facial contortions or body movements. You are not, however, required to remain motionless. Some exhibitors cross their arms when they are facing their dogs on this exercise as an extra, legal reminder to the dog to remain in place.

Listen to the judge's instructions before you leave your dog. He or she will tell you what to do if your dog breaks position and comes to you or goes to another dog.

If Your Dog Breaks Position

Listen to the judge's instructions before you leave your dog. He or she will tell you what to do if your dog breaks position and comes to you or goes to another dog. You may be told to retrieve your dog yourself on the judge's order, or the steward may bring the dog to you to hold. If so, do not correct the dog (tempting though it may

Be sure that your dog is sitting up squarely. The setter is slouching, and the silky terrier is not sitting squarely. Both dogs are more likely to lie down than the dogs on the ends of the line.

be), but tell him to sit and stay in front of you. Do not unthinkingly pet the dog, because this may encourage him to repeat the behavior. The judge may have the steward hold the dog at the side of the ring.

If Your Dog Lies Down or Stands Up

If the dog lies down or stands up as you give him the "stay" command, you may want to give a verbal command to sit, or you may even want to gently reposition him. If he completes the rest of the exercise successfully, the judge may give him a qualifying score. This is another individual judgment call. If your dog stands or lies down after you have left him, there is nothing that you can do about it. Under any circumstances, do *not* physically correct him when you return. If the dog changes position after you have returned to heel position, he will pass, but with a substantial deduction. If, however, you are even one step away from heel position when he breaks, he will fail.

You are not required to break your dog from position at the end of the Long Sit. Some trainers point out that it is not a good idea to excite the dog at the end of the sit and then require him to lie quietly for three minutes. On the other hand, some dogs get in the habit of lying down the moment the Long Sit is over, in anticipation of the Long Down. This can become a serious problem when the dog makes his own decision about when the Long Sit is finished.

Proofing the Long Sit

Dogs with Physical Problems/Laziness. Some dogs seem to have innate difficulties maintaining the sit position. They may be short-coated, thin-skinned dogs (whippets and chihuahuas) or dogs with bad hips, for whom the Long Sit may be somewhat uncomfortable. Or, they may be lazy louts that would rather lie down and sleep than sit up for one to three minutes.

Some of these dogs are surprisingly devious and manage to save this behavior for the show ring, never failing to hold the sit in practice. Discuss corrections for this problem with your instructor, but also consider the following:

If your dog lies down or stands up as you give him the "stay" command, you may want to give a verbal command to sit, or gently reposition him. If he completes the rest of the exercise successfully, the judge may give him a qualifying score. If your dog stands or lies down after you have left him, he fails. Do NOT physically correct him when you return. You are not required to break your dog from position at the end of the Long Sit.

Some dogs have innate difficulties maintaining the sit position. They may be short-coated, thin-skinned dogs or dogs with bad hips. Or, they may be lazy louts!

To proof the Long Sit, practice sit-stays longer than the requisite one or three minutes. Be sure to leave your dog in a good sit position.

1. Practice sit-stays longer than the requisite one or three minutes. If your dog can sit for five to seven minutes, the shorter time in the ring will be a cinch.
2. Be sure to leave your dog in a good sit position (but remember *not to adjust him in the ring* — work this out in training).

A dog that starts out slouching will be more likely to lie down than one that is sitting up smartly.

Proof against temptation on the ground with food, toys, etc. as described in the heeling section.

Smells. Interesting smells on the ground can also lure first the nose and then the entire body down. Proof against this with food, toys, etc. as described in the heeling section. A dog that sniffs repeatedly should lose points, even if he does not lie down.

Other Dogs Lying Down. A dog may also lie down when the dog next to him in line does so. Practice having your dog hold a sit while the next dog is told to lie down. Frequently, two rings will have stays going on simultaneously, with the lines of dogs back to back. Be sure that your dog will not be bothered by having other dogs only a few feet behind him, and that he will not lie down when the handlers in the adjacent ring give a "down" command.

Be sure that your dog will not be bothered by having other dogs only a few feet behind him, and that he will not lie down when the handlers in the adjacent ring give a "down" command. Distractions may also cause a dog to break the Long Sit. Noises can startle or attract a dog that is supposed to be sitting still.

Distractions. Distractions may also cause a dog to break the Long Sit. In addition to food or interesting smells, noises can startle or attract a dog that is supposed to be sitting still. Spectators may drag chairs or baby strollers behind the line of sitting dogs. Children running loose may grab the ring gates and shake them.

I once judged one of my student's dogs at a fun match. During the Long Down in Open, a strong wind came up and blew over the ring barrier. Before anyone could act, the gate fell on the dog's rump. This dog had been so strongly proofed on the stays that he never moved a muscle except to turn his head and give me a dirty look, certain that I had set up another proofing situation to test his steadiness. The dog was not hurt, and I was happy to see that he had really learned the meaning of "stay." He had been proofed against so many odd things that he took this incident in stride.

Proofing the sit stay. These dogs are not being distracted by activity in the ring behind them (and vice versa for the retrieving dog).

On another occasion, a child was climbing on a chair next to the ring, lost his balance, and fell into the ring during a stay exercise. Some of the dogs stayed, and some did not. The judge did not rejudge those that left because some dogs did hold position. Judges and stewards should be alert to these distractions and stop them before they disturb the dog, but don't count on it.

Activity in the Adjoining Ring. Be sure that legitimate activity in the adjoining ring does not cause your dog to move. Have someone practice recalls and retrieves behind your dog to simulate this type of situation.

Noises/Weather Variations. Speak to your instructor, or use your ingenuity, to accustom your dog to all types of noises, from dropped chairs to fire alarms. If you plan to show outside frequently, practice stays in the sun, wind, and rain. Also practice working in total silence. Often at a trial, things may suddenly become very quiet

Set up all kinds of disturbances and train your dog to ignore them.

Be sure that legitimate activity in the adjoining ring does not cause your dog to move. Have someone practice recalls and retrieves behind your dog. Accustom your dog to all types of noises, and practice stays in the sun, wind, and rain. Practice working in total silence.

and dogs will relax. Then, there will be a sudden loud noise (a slamming door or a baby crying), and the dogs will be startled from their somnolent state and jump up out of position.

Keep your dog guessing as to what will happen when you return to him on this exercise so that he does not start anticipating the Long Down. Do not always follow a sit-stay with a down-stay.

When You Return to Your Dog. It is a good idea to keep the dog guessing as to what will happen when you return to him on this exercise so that he does not start anticipating the Long Down. Vary your routine in practice and at fun matches by leaving again after returning, or circling the dog an extra time. Do not always follow a sit-stay with a down-stay.

It is my belief that dogs should be trained to permit themselves to be led away from a stay group by a stranger. This is especially important if you have a shy or aggressive dog.

Training Your Dog to Be Led Away By a Stranger. I am now going to discuss an issue that some readers will find controversial; nevertheless, it is important. It is my belief that dogs should be trained to permit themselves to be led away from a stay group by a stranger. This is especially important if you have a shy or aggressive dog. As a judge, I have seen far too many dogs that had made mistakes on the group exercises (leaving their places or going to another dog) and that would not allow a steward to touch them. This is more of an issue in the Open classes, when the handlers are gone, but I have seen Novice classes in which the dog's own handler could not catch the animal. I once saw a Tervuren clear an entire group of twelve Novice A dogs out of the stay line before his owner was able to catch him. I have also had the unfortunate experience of having a dog bite a steward who was trying (in a totally non-threatening manner) to remove the dog from the middle of the ring.

In my training classes, we practice having other people deliberately remove dogs from the line (sometimes by putting on the leash and walking away with the dog). This may not seem quite fair to you, but it teaches the dogs that they may not bite or run away when approached by a stranger during a stay and has probably prevented a number of aggressive dogs from being permanently disqualified for biting or attempting to bite under these conditions. It is an adjunct to our other proofing. The dogs learn to ignore just about any temptation to move from position. We have used all types of food and toys, a mechanical cat that makes noise and rolls around, and people crawling around making strange noises. We get some funny looks, but our dogs are pretty reliable on the stays.

Common Handling Errors

The most common handling errors committed on the Long Sit include the handler:

- Physically positioning the dog before the exercise.
- Giving loud commands.
- Using body English to make the dog stay.
- Failing to return all the way to heel position.

Pass or Fail?

If the dog remained in the sitting position from the time you left until you were securely back in heel position without repeatedly barking or whining and without moving a body length, he probably passed.

The Long Down

There is no regulation prohibiting or penalizing a repeated command to down, and no dog should lose points for requiring two commands and a hand signal before complying.

However, there are times when the dog has clearly decided not to cooperate. If your dog refuses to lie down after you have given him several verbal commands, take hold of his collar and gently put him down. You will lose some points but will not fail.

If your dog lies down at an angle so that he might interfere with another dog, the judge will ask you to reposition him and will deduct three or more points. If this occurs, go ahead and use your hands (remember to be gentle) to straighten the dog, because the points are already lost and other exhibitors are waiting to proceed with the exercise.

It is a good idea to teach your dog to lie down in a consistent manner, next to your left leg. The bigger the dog, the more critical this becomes, as you can see in the photo. Many trainers insist that the dog always assume a particular position for the Long Down. Ask your instructor about this.

Common Handling Errors

- *Physically positioning the dog before the exercise.*
- *Giving loud commands.*
- *Using body English to make the dog stay.*
- *Failing to return all the way to heel position.*

Pass

- *If the dog remained in the sitting position from the time you left until you were securely back in heel position without repeatedly barking or whining and without moving a body length.*

If your dog refuses to lie down after you have given him several verbal commands, take hold of his collar and gently put him down. You will lose some points but will not fail.

It is a good idea to teach your dog to lie down in a consistent manner, next to your left leg. The bigger the dog, the more critical this becomes.

These three dogs are in essentially the same down position, but the dog on the left, because of its size, is going to have to be repositioned and will be hit with a substantial deduction. The bigger the dog, the more it matters HOW it lies down.

If the dog next to yours has changed position, return around BOTH dogs, rather than attempting to wedge or vault between them.

No judge should let two dogs get this close on the Long Down, but if it happens to you and you can't get between them to return to heel position, try to put at least one foot in the heel position to show that you do know where you're supposed to be.

If your dog or the dog next to him rolls over when there is not much space between dogs, you may find that you cannot return to heel position without stepping over one or both dogs. In that case, return around **both** dogs so that you do not have to step over either dog. If there is no room between your dog and the dog to his left for you to stand next to your dog in the heel position, get as close as you can without stepping over either dog. Ideally, an alert judge will not permit two dogs to roll that close to each other and will remove one or both of them to prevent possible trouble.

Be sure to put your dog's leash back on before leaving the group line.

Proofing the Long Down

Proofing for this exercise is almost identical to that used for the Long Sit. Be sure that your dog does not flop around during this exercise, because he may easily

If your dog or the dog next to him rolls over when there is not much space between dogs, you may not be able to return to heel position without stepping over one or both dogs. In that case, return around both dogs. If there is no room between your dog and the dog to his left for you to stand next to your dog in the heel position, get as close as you can without stepping over either dog.

Common Handling
Errors

- *Revving up the dog
  after the Long Sit so
  that he is too excited
  to lie down promptly.*
- *Allowing the dog to lie
  down at an angle.*
- *Physically putting the
  dog down.*

Pass

- *If your dog remained in
  the down position
  for the full three
  minutes, without
  repeatedly barking or
  whining.*

Fail

- *If your dog stayed down
  but crawled or rolled a
  significant distance
  from his original spot.*
- *If your dog got up.*

*If your dog has qualified,
take him out for a last
exercise break as the class
is ending. Give him a
drink and wake him up
for a potential run-off.*

flop too far and be removed for getting too close to another dog. Most judges will tolerate a minor position change, such as shifting from one hip to the other, but a dog that is in constant motion will lose points or even fail the exercise.

The dog will be even closer to fascinating smells on this exercise, so work hard to teach him not to be tempted to investigate. Also, be sure that he will lie down readily on wet grass or cold concrete.

Common Handling Errors

Common handling errors for the Long Down include the following:

- Revving up the dog after the Long Sit.
- Not teaching the dog to lie down straight and then having to reposition him in the exercise.
- Physically putting the dog down; however, as discussed earlier, this may actually be considered "good" handling if your dog refuses cooperate.

Pass or Fail?

If your dog remained in the down position for the full three minutes, without repeatedly barking or whining, he probably passed. If he stayed down but crawled or rolled a significant distance from his original spot, he will probably not pass. Remember — when this exercise is finished, the judge will come around and tell you if you have qualified or not.

The End of the Class

Exercise Break

If your dog has qualified, take him out for a last exercise break as the class is ending, while the last group exercise is underway. Give him a drink and wake him up with whatever your normal warm-up routine is. No matter how you think your dog performed, wake him up for a potential run-off. You can never predict what a judge may have thought about your performance.

Run-Offs

If you have tied for a placement in the class, or for a breed trophy (e.g., highest scoring fuzzy terrier in Novice B), you will be called by armband number to come to the ring for a run-off. This will consist of an off-lead heeling pattern for each dog, individually, generally in catalogue order. If the dogs in the run-off receive the same score on the heeling pattern, they will have to do it again and possibly even a third time.

The judge may or may not announce the winner on the spot. When the run-offs are complete, all of the qualifying dogs will be called back into the ring, and scores and placements will be announced. If you and your dog have won first prize in your class, *do not leave the show,* because you may be highest scoring in trial (unless another class has also ended and the winner had a higher score than yours). If a trophy was listed for which you are eligible, check to see if others are also competing for it. If so, you must wait until every eligible handler's score has been awarded to know if you have won. Trophies (other than class placements) are almost always awarded at the end of the trial after all judging is completed. Occasionally, there are run-offs for these trophies and for Highest Scoring Dog in Trial. These run-offs take place right before final awards are made at the end of the trial or show.

If you have tied for a placement in the class, or for a breed trophy, you will be called by armband number to come to the ring for a run-off. This will consist of an off-lead heeling pattern for each dog, individually, generally in catalogue order.

If you and your dog have won first prize in your class, do not leave *the show, because you may be highest scoring in trial. If a trophy was listed for which you are eligible, check to see if others are also competing for it. If so, you must wait until every eligible handler's score has been awarded to know if you have won.*

Photographs

If your dog has some something special — earned his first leg, completed a title, won a special award — you should commemorate the occasion by having a picture taken. The steward can call for the show photographer, and you will pose with the judge, the dog, and any trophies or ribbons you have won. The photographer will make note of your armband number and send the picture to you through the mail. If you like the picture, you pay for it by return mail. If you are not satisfied, you may return the picture to the photographer by mail. A few photographers collect their fees on the spot, so be prepared to pay.

If your dog has done something special, have a picture taken to commemorate the occasion.

Go to the superintendent's table to check your score before leaving the show grounds. Be sure that your score was added correctly and that the score listed agrees with the score given to you by the judge earlier. If there is a discrepancy, bring it to the attention of the superintendent immediately.

Checking Your Score

Get in the habit of going over to the superintendent's table to check your score before you leave the show grounds. There will be a copy of the judge's book (in which he marked the scores) available for you to see. Be sure that your score was added correctly and that the score listed agrees with the score given to you by the judge earlier. If you notice a discrepancy, immediately bring it to the attention of the superintendent. Some exhibitors make a habit of writing down how many points they have lost on each exercise for future reference.

Thoughts on Scores

Remember that your score is nothing more than one judge's opinion of your dog's performance on a particular day. It has no effect on your dog's affection for you and does not mark your dog as good or bad. *It should not affect your relationship with your dog.*

If you feel that your dog unjustly received a non-qualifying score or if a judge deducted points that made no sense to you, you may approach the judge and politely ask about the score. You may not argue with the judge. If the judge has time, he or she will usually be willing to explain the decision. If you still feel that the judge was in error or inaccurate, you can speak to the AKC field representative at the show and register a polite complaint. This will not result in your score being changed. It is my opinion that a competent judge should be able to tell you why a deduction was made, even at the end of a large class.

Sometimes, however, there are discrepancies that you will want to address. If you feel that your dog unjustly received a non-qualifying score or if a judge deducted points for something that makes no sense to you, you may approach the judge and *politely* ask about the score. *You may not argue with the judge.* It may be that you have misunderstood the regulations pertaining to a particular exercise, or inadvertently made a handling error. Maintain the attitude that you are asking for information and not defending your honor. If the judge has time, he or she will usually be willing to explain the decision. The judge is encouraged but not required by the AKC to do so. Remember that judges make mistakes and that scores, once recorded in the judge's book, cannot be changed except to correct computational errors.

If, after discussing the matter calmly, you still feel that the judge was in error or inaccurate, or even unfair, there is really nothing that you can do about the particular score in question. Judges' decisions are always final.

You can, however, take some action to express your dissatisfaction. You can speak to the AKC field representative at the show and register a polite complaint. This will not result in your score being changed. A more effec-

If the dog has done something memorable, have a picture taken. Here, judge Nancy Pollock, with infinite good taste, was awarding us a High in Trial.

tive protest would consist of a polite, reasonably worded letter, outlining the situation as you see it, addressed to the director of obedience, with copies to the show-giving club and to the judge with whom you are in dispute. Do not write a poison-pen letter, but have the courage to bring your charges directly to the people involved. If the judge was truly in error, the AKC will address the issue. If it was a matter of incompetence or deliberate unpleasantness on the part of the judge, and if several people have written similar letters, the club will be unlikely to hire that judge again. Furthermore, word gets around in a given area, and the judge will receive fewer and fewer invitations to officiate. Judges are evaluated regularly by AKC field representatives and are given feedback to improve their performances and to standardize judging.

Don't waste too much energy feeling victimized by a score lower than you felt you deserved. These things tend to balance out, and for every low score you get, you will likely receive a gift of a higher score than you deserved.

Don't waste too much energy feeling victimized by a score lower than you felt you deserved. These things tend to balance out, and for every low score you get, you will be likely to receive a gift of a higher score than you deserved. These "gift" scores are fun to receive because they are generally unexpected.

On one occasion, my Open dog decided that a particular judge was going to do terrible things to him. During the performance, the dog left heel position at least three times (I stopped looking after that). The front sits were all crooked because the dog was watching the judge over his shoulder. The finishes were crooked because the dog was trying to hide behind me. He received a score of 198 and second prize. The next day, the dog gave me one of the very best performances of his career but received a low score and did not place. The lesson I learned from that weekend was to accept the low scores philosophically and to enjoy the "gift" scores without apologizing to anybody. Keeping your perspective is one of the best lessons the obedience ring can teach you.

Observing Cheating

A last word before moving on to the Open exercises. If you are absolutely certain that a fellow exhibitor has cheated in some way (double handling on group exercises, using food in the ring), it is not up to you to discipline the cheater. You may report the incident to the judge, who may or may not choose to act on your report. If you can prove your accusations or have corroboration from other exhibitors, you can take your concerns to the obedience chairperson of the club, who can invoke the powers of the trial committee as described on page 34. You should do the same thing if you see someone abusing a dog.

If you are absolutely certain that a fellow exhibitor has cheated, report the incident to the judge, or the obedience chairperson.

■

In the Open Ring

Once you have received three qualifying scores from three different judges in Novice A or B, and if your dog is ready, you may enter him in Open. You do not have to wait to receive your Companion Dog certificate from the AKC.

Now that you have advanced beyond the Novice level, you will find that there are a few changes in the ring procedures:

- In the Open and the Utility ring, you may not touch your dog or his collar to correct or guide him.
- You may still pet him between exercises.
- You must have voice control of your dog.
- If you have an exuberant dog, be especially careful that he doesn't get too excited between exercises, because you will lose points (but should still qualify) if you have to control him physically at any time.

All of the information regarding handling the dog on the Novice Recall applies equally to Open exercises in which the dog comes to you:

- You must stand still with your hands hanging naturally at your sides.
- The Heel Free is the same as in Novice, except that the Figure 8 is done off leash.
- Review the warm-up rules in the Novice section. You may *not* practice jumping, retrieving, or drops as part of your pre–Open warm-up routine.
- Be sure to move your dog around enough to loosen him up before entering the ring. This will help prepare him for the jumping exercises to come.

Measuring

Once you have received
three qualifying scores
and your dog is ready, you
may enter him in Open.
There are several changes
in ring procedure:
- *You may not touch your*
  dog or his collar to
  position or guide him.
- *You must have voice*
  control of your dog.
- *You will lose points if*
  you have to control
  your dog physically at
  any time.

When you check in at your
ring, be prepared to
report your jump heights
to the steward, who will
mark them in the
catalogue. Do not expect
the stewards to calculate
this for you.

Train your dog to stand
for measuring as though
it were a separate Open
exercise. When you hold
your dog for measuring,
you may do it from the
front or the side. Hold
your dog's head level
rather then up. After the
dog has been measured,
check the jumps to see
that they are set properly
before beginning the
heeling pattern.

When you check in at your ring, be prepared to report your jump heights to the steward, who will mark them in the catalogue. Do not expect the stewards to calculate this for you. If your dog measures on the borderline between two jump heights (that is, if some people measure him at 23¾ inches and others measure him right at 24 inches), there is nothing wrong in reporting the lower heights to the steward. The judge will measure your dog and make his or her own determination. If you have such a dog, you would do well to practice with him at both possible jump heights. This is especially important if either measurement results in a change in the number of boards used in the broad jump. A four-board jump looks very different to a dog from a three-board jump, even though the total distance changed amounts to only four inches.

Train your dog to stand for measuring as though it were a separate Open exercise. Even the most stable dog may become unnerved when he sees a stranger approaching him with a stick. It is acceptable and advisable to hold your dog while he is being measured in case the judge is a bit clumsy with the measuring tape or otherwise disturbs the dog. If your dog is upset by the measuring process, it is likely to have a negative effect on his entire performance. If the dog actively resists being measured, the judge is within his or her rights to excuse the dog.

When you hold your dog for measuring, you may do it from the front or the side. I advise my students to hold their dogs' heads level rather than up (see the photos). If your dog is on the borderline for a specific jump height, holding his head up can raise his shoulders, resulting in a higher measurement.

If your dog is shy or just does not like being approached with a stick, try an old trick used by professional breed handlers, and cover the dog's eyes as the judge approaches. This helps some dogs remain calm.

After the dog has been measured, check the jumps to see that they are set properly before beginning the heeling pattern.

Holding the dog this way for measuring looks very pretty but may raise the height of the withers and cause the dog to have to jump an extra four inches.

A better way to hold the dog for measuring: The handler has her hands securely on the dog and is holding the head down slightly to flatten the withers.

Open Individual Exercises

The Heel Free exercise is identical to the Novice Heel Free except that the Figure 8 is also done off leash.

Drop on Recall

One of the choices that an exhibitor must make is whether to use a verbal command or a hand signal to down his or her dog. There are no regulations affecting this choice except that you cannot use both.

Many dogs respond better to a signal than to a voice command. On the other hand, a dog has a harder time ignoring a voice command than pretending he did not see a signal. Many dogs manage to ignore both, of course. Check with your instructor and then consider the ring conditions on any particular day. If it is very noisy, a signal may be in order. If the dog is especially distractable, the verbal command may be more compelling.

If you do use a hand signal, the AKC *Regulations* permit only two types:

- You may either extend your hand and arm straight up in the air and then *immediately* drop them to your side, or
- You may make a circular motion, bringing your extended arm up and around from back to front.

In either case, the movement must be continuous, with no pause at the top. Such a pause constitutes a double command and will cause you to fail the exercise. Only the arm may move; any bending at the neck or waist will be penalized.

Similarly, an excessively loud or nasty command will be penalized. Your tone of voice and volume level should be the same for the recall and drop portions of the exercise. If your dog fails to drop on the first command or signal, I would recommend that you repeat it, because you have nothing further to lose (the judge can't give you less than a zero for the exercise). If you don't step toward the dog, it is unlikely that the judge will excuse you for making the correction, but it is possible.

You may use either a verbal command or a hand signal to down your dog, but you cannot use both. Only two types of hand signals are permitted:
- *Extending your hand and arm straight up in the air and then immediately dropping them to your side, or*
- *Making a circular motion, bringing your extended arm up and around from back to front.*
In either case, the movement must be continuous, with no pause at the top.

If your dog fails to drop on the first command or signal, I recommend that you repeat it, because you have nothing to lose (the judge can't give you less than a zero for the exercise). Your drop command should be identical in tone and volume to your recall command.

Proofing the Drop on Recall

Proof the recall portion as outlined for the Novice Recall. There are a number of different elements involved in proofing the Drop:

- Don't always drop your dog at the same distance when you practice. Sometimes, call him and drop him after he has taken only two steps. Other times, drop him almost at your feet. Ocasionally, return and free the dog.
- Set up visual and auditory distractions to be sure that the dog will drop no matter what else is going on.
- Try turning your back to the dog and giving the drop command or signal. This will tell you if your dog truly understands the Drop.

In proofing the Drop:
- *Don't always drop your dog at the same distance when you practice.*
- *Set up visual and auditory distractions.*
- *Try turning your back to the dog and giving the drop command or signal.*
- *Vary the exercise by frequently returning to the dog after he has dropped and freeing him or heeling him off.*

Common Handling Errors

Common handling errors for the Drop on Recall include the following:

- Pausing at the top of the hand signal, which constitutes a double command.
- Bending at the neck or waist when giving the hand signal.
- Giving excessively loud or nasty commands.

Common Handling Errors
- *Pausing at the top of the hand signal, which constitutes a double command.*
- *Bending at the neck or waist when giving the hand signal.*
- *Giving excessively loud or nasty commands.*

Pass or Fail?

The standards are identical to those for the Novice Recall. In addition, the dog must not drop before the command or signal is given and must wait to be called the second time without getting up from the down position. Points are deducted for slow responses to any of these commands.

Pass
- *See Novice Recall.*
- *If the dog does not drop before the signal or command is given.*
- *If the dog drops completely (elbows and rump).*
- *If the dog waits to be called the second time without getting up from the down position.*

Criteria For A Good Drop

How fast does the dog have to drop? It's relative. I once judged a beautiful champion Rough Collie that came like a bullet when called. When given the drop signal, he simply folded his legs in midair and hit the deck. It

- *If the dog responds immediately to the command or signal, moving forward no more than one body length before being down completely.*
- *If the dog's down is a continuous motion.*
- *The dog that moves forward more than a body length or drops in segments should lose points.*

The dumbbell for the Retrieve on the Flat must be proportionate to the size of the dog. Allow one-half-inch clearance between the dog's lip and the bell. The bells should be just tall enough so that the dog can pick the dumbbell up without bumping his nose or scraping his underjaw on the ground.

The bells may be round or square. Many exhibitors paint the bells of the dumbbells white to increase visibility for the dog.

was a spectacular sight (although a bit wearing on the dog's elbows, I would fear), but not every dog is required to drop in that manner.

As a judge, I consider it to be a good drop when the dog responds immediately to the command or signal, moving forward no more than one body length before being down completely. I also expect the down to be a continuous motion, not a sit followed by a pause before the elbows hit the ground. Huskies and Samoyeds are famous for the opposite behavior: the elbows go down promptly, but the rump remains in the air for a second or two.

Retrieve on the Flat

The Dumbbell

Size. The *Regulations* state that the dumbbell must be proportionate to the size of the dog. This means that the dowel should be long enough to allow the dog to hold it comfortably without pinching his lips. A dowel that is too long encourages the dog to mouth the dumbbell to keep it balanced. A good rule of thumb is to allow one-half-inch clearance between the dog's lip and the bell. This means that dogs with long flews (Bassets and most Setters, among others) need a longer dowel than tight-lipped breeds like Dobermans and spitz-type dogs. Square-faced dogs or those with undershot jaws (such as Pugs, Bostons, and Bulldogs) also need longer dowels. The bells should be just tall enough so that the dog can pick the dumbbell up without bumping his nose or scraping his underjaw on the ground.

Shape/Color. The bells may be round or square. Most exhibitors find it easier to throw the square-ended dumbbells accurately because they do not roll as badly as the round ones. Check with your instructor. Many exhibitors paint the bells of the dumbbell white to increase visibility for the dog.

How Many to Carry. Always carry at least two, and preferably three, dumbbells in case one breaks in the ring. One of your spares should be darker in color, to use on a light-colored floor. Take two dumbbells to the

This dog is holding a correctly fitted dumbbell. He can close his mouth over it, the ends do not obscure his vision, and it is tall enough for him to pick up without bumping his nose on the ground. The ends are painted white for visibility.

Same dog, but the dumbbell is too large. His vision is partially blocked and he cannot close his mouth.

Always carry at least two, and preferably three, dumbbells in case one breaks in the ring. One of your spares should be darker in color, to use on a light-colored floor.

If your dog has chewed up the dowel of your practice dumbbell in training, get an additional unchewed dumbbell to use in the ring. Handing the judge a chewed dumbbell in the ring unnecessarily telegraphs your training problem.

Practice throwing the dumbbell so that you can place it to your dog's advantage in the ring. Keep it away from a spot where another dog fouled the ring or an area at ringside where spectators are noisily eating lunch.

Practice having to rethrow the dumbbell with your dog. Some dogs have a problem anticipating the retrieve in case of a rethrow. The judge will decide if the dumbbell needs to be rethrown. Keep your dog under control while the judge goes to retrieve the dumbbell.

ring, put them on the judge's table, and tell the steward which you want to use first. Have the other spare at your seat.

Plastic Dumbbells. The new plastic dumbbells are nice, because they are nearly unbreakable. I find that they bounce more erratically than the wooden ones, however.

If Your Dog Chews the Dowel. If your dog has chewed up the dowel of your practice dumbbell in training, get an additional unchewed dumbbell to use in the ring. Ask your instructor how to stop the dog from chewing and mouthing the dumbbell. Be sure that the dog has had a few opportunities to retrieve the new dumbbell so that it is not strange to him in the ring. Handing the judge a chewed dumbbell in the ring unnecessarily telegraphs your training problem and could cause the judge to watch more closely to catch the dog mouthing the dumbbell and make a deduction.

Throwing the Dumbbell. It is important that you practice throwing the dumbbell so that you can place it to your dog's advantage in the ring. Ideally, the dog should retrieve under any circumstances, but it is helpful to keep him away from a spot where another dog fouled the ring (an invitation to sniff, or worse) or an area at ringside where spectators are noisily eating lunch. (If such people are especially close to the ring barrier, you may ask the steward to request that they move a bit further away before you enter the ring.)

Rethrows. Be sure to practice having to rethrow the dumbbell with your dog. Some dogs have a problem with anticipating the retrieve in case of a rethrow. The judge will decide if the dumbbell needs to be rethrown. Keep your dog under control while the judge goes to retrieve the dumbbell. It is usually not a good idea to release the dog, because he may head for the dumbbell and lose points for being out of control, or be failed for anticipating the retrieve. I once had a dog knock me down and try to wrest his dumbbell from me as I was returning it for a rethrow.

The "Mark." Many exhibitors like to give their dog a look at the dumbell (also known as a "mark") before they throw it. This serves to focus the dog's attention so that he will follow the dumbbell with his eyes to the spot where it lands. The mark must be given before you tell the judge that you are ready. You may not give your stay signal with the hand that is holding the dumbbell. Do not move your feet after throwing the dumbbell, and stand still as the dog is returning to you.

The mark must be given before you tell the judge that you are ready. You may not give your stay signal with the hand that is holding the dumbbell. Do not move your feet after throwing the dumbbell, and stand still as the dog is returning to you.

Handicapped Handlers. Handicapped handlers who cannot throw the dumbbell the required twenty-foot distance may leave the dog at the place where the exercise begins, proceed away from the dog however far they must go, then throw (not drop) the dumbbell. They then return to heel position and proceed with the retrieve exercise in the usual manner.

Handicapped handlers who cannot throw the dumbbell twenty feet may leave the dog where the exercise begins, proceed away from the dog however far they must go, then throw (not drop) the dumbbell.

Proofing the Retrieve on the Flat

Several elements of this exercise must be proofed:

- The stay.
- The pick-up.
- The direction the dog travels.

The Stay. Proofing against anticipation is especially important for the more maniacal retrievers (Labs, Goldens, Border Collies) that are on a hair-trigger on this exercise. Teach the dog to go only on the command word. Try saying words that sound a bit like the command word ("Rover, fool" instead of "Rover, fetch"), and restrain or correct the dog for not waiting for the correct term. Throw the dumbbell and retrieve it yourself. Or, throw the dumbbell and heel the dog off in the other direction. As in the Novice Recall, take a deep breath, twitch your arms, flex your knees, and make the dog wait. Have someone else say, "Send your dog," or say it yourself.

To proof against anticipation, teach your dog to go only on the command word.

The Pick-Up. Be sure that the dog makes a clean pick-up, rather than dropping the dumbbell habitually, hitting it with his feet, or otherwise not attending directly to the business at hand. Have the dog retrieve around

Be sure that your dog makes a clean pick-up rather than dropping the dumbbell habitually, or hitting it with his feet.

Have your dog retrieve around distractions, and make sure that he will retrieve the dumbbell from any surface, including wet grass or mud.

distractions, including food, toys, children, other dogs, and anything else you can devise.

The dog should retrieve the dumbbell from any surface, including wet grass or mud. If you have a small dog, teach him to mark where the dumbbell lands and to keep searching until the dumbbell is found, even in tall grass. The continuous searching is important for larger dogs as well. In practice, we put the dumbbell up on chairs and hang it in bushes, and the dog gets the message that he must not come back without it. Prepare your dog for the one in a hundred times the dumbbell lands on end rather than flat.

Proof against your dog jumping the high jump by throwing the dumbbell alongside the jump and teaching your dog to ignore the jump unless the dumbbell is thrown over it.

Jumping the High Jump. Ideally, the dog should go straight out to the dumbbell, pick it up, and bring it directly back. In a small ring, many green Open dogs will jump the high jump in one or both directions during the Retrieve on the Flat. While this will cost you a substantial deduction, it is not an automatic failure. Proof against this by throwing the dumbbell alongside the jump and teaching the dog to ignore the jump unless the dumbbell is thrown over it. Some trainers use different commands for the Retrieve on the Flat and the Retrieve Over the High Jump to help the dog understand the difference.

Common Handling Errors

- *Giving the stay with the hand holding the dumbbell.*
- *Not throwing the dumbbell at least twenty feet.*
- *Dropping the dumbbell.*
- *Moving your feet after sending your dog.*

Common Handling Errors

Common handling errors for the Retrieve on the Flat include:

- Giving the stay with the hand holding the dumbbell.
- Not throwing the dumbbell at least twenty feet.
- Dropping the dumbbell.
- Moving your feet after sending the dog.

Pass

- *If your dog waited for the retrieve command.*
- *If your dog went out on your first command.*

(Continued on next page)

Pass or Fail?

If your dog waited for the retrieve command, went out on your first command, picked up the dumbbell, and brought it back within an arm's length of you, he probably passed.

Dogs commonly lose points for moving slowly, not going directly to the dumbbell or returning directly to the handler, dropping the dumbbell, or mouthing it. A dog that hits the dumbbell with his feet before picking it up will lose points. No regulation requires a deduction for picking up the dumbbell by the end rather than by the dowel. Touching the handler with the dumbbell while sitting in front is also a reason for a minor deduction.

As mentioned in the Proofing section, dogs that are new to the Open ring will frequently jump over the high jump in one or both directions in the course of this exercise. This is especially likely if the ring is small and/or the handler throws the dumbbell close to the jump. This calls for a substantial penalty for not returning directly but should *not* result in a non-qualifying score.

A dog that drops the dumbbell at any time will be penalized. If he drops it in front of the handler, it must be within the handler's reach (without the handler having to move either foot) to qualify. If the handler drops the dumbbell (and I have — right on the dog's head), most judges will make a deduction for a handling error.

- *If your dog picked up the dumbbell and brought it back within an arm's length of you.*

Lose Points

- *Moving slowly.*
- *Not going directly to the dumbbell or returning directly to the handler.*
- *Dropping or mouthing the dumbbell.*
- *Hitting the dumbbell with the feet before picking it up.*
- *Touching the handler with the dumbbell while sitting in front.*
- *Jumping over the high jump in one or both directions in the course of the exercise.*

Retrieve Over the High Jump

All of the discussion of the Retrieve on the Flat pertains equally to this exercise; however, there are some additional considerations regarding the high jump.

Distance from the Jump

You and the dog must stand at least eight feet back from the jump. Frequently, the judge will have drawn some sort of line on the floor or mat at the eight-foot mark. Many dogs, however, do better if given more room to run up to the jump. You may want to experiment with your dog to see what distance is best for him. You can frequently get as far as fifteen feet or more from the jump. If you have trouble judging distance visually, you can simply figure out ahead of time how many steps you must take to measure off the desired distance, and then, while in the ring, unobtrusively pace off that number of steps before facing the jump.

You can also pace off this distance from outside the ring and make a mental note of some point of reference

For the Retrieve Over the High Jump, you and the dog must stand at least eight feet back from the jump. Many dogs do better if given more room to run up to the jump. Experiment with your dog to see what distance is best for him. You can frequently get as far as fifteen feet or more from the jump.

with which you will align yourself before the exercise. This can be more challenging than it sounds. At one trial, the exhibitor who was first in Open B had carefully paced off the appropriate distance as the judge was setting up the ring. She went to get her dog to do a brief warm-up. When she came back, she realized that the judge had rearranged the ring — so she paced off her distance again. Then, before the judge called the exhibitor into the ring, she changed her mind again and directed the stewards to reposition the jumps. The poor exhibitor was now totally confused and unable to remember which reference points were accurate. When she came out of the ring, she told us that she had given up and just guessed at the correct distances.

Placement in Front of the Jump

Discover whether your dog does better when you center him in front of the jump, or when you center yourself.

You must also discover whether your dog does better when you center **him** in front of the jump, or when you center **yourself.** In the former case, some dogs will be less likely to run around the left side of the jump. Centering yourself, however, increases the odds for a straight sit in front. Handlers have a tendency to move their feet after sending the dog for the dumbbell. As in the Recall, this is a handling error. Adjust your position before you tell the judge that you are ready, then stand still.

Throwing Accuracy

The accuracy of your throw is important. It may mean the difference between the dog's passing or failing.

As in the Retrieve on the Flat, the accuracy of your throw is important. In fact, it may mean the difference between the dog's passing or failing. Most dogs will consistently turn in one direction (right or left) after picking up the dumbbell and before coming back to you. If your dog turns to the right and you have thrown the dumbbell to the right of the jump, the dog will be looking directly at you rather than at the jump when he turns after picking up the dumbbell. He is more likely to bypass the jump on the return than if you had centered your throw or even thrown a bit toward the left. Observe your dog, and take his turn direction into consideration. You should, of course, proof train your dog to jump in both directions, no matter where the dumbbell lands. Discuss this with your instructor. You must throw the dumbbell at least eight feet beyond the jump.

Observe your dog and take his turn direction into consideration. You should, of course, proof train your dog to jump in both directions, no matter where the dumbbell lands. You must throw the dumbbell at least eight feet beyond the jump.

If Your Dog Climbs the Jump

A dog that climbs the jump — that is, puts his front or back feet on top of the jump and pushes off — will fail this exercise. A dog that merely touches the jump, even if it is a hard touch, will probably not fail but will lose points. If your dog hits the jump hard enough to knock it over, he will also fail. Dogs that do not jump smoothly — that "stutter" jump or show hesitation or reluctance to jump — will lose points, even if they clear the jump successfully.

Proofing the Retrieve Over the High Jump

Correcting the Retrieve Portion. Many problems associated with the retrieving portion of this exercise are the result of inadequate training of the Retrieve on the Flat. Analyze your dog's problem and correct the retrieve before worrying about the jumping portion. Proofing for the retrieve portion has already been described.

Physical Problems. Some dogs are physically unable to clear the jumps because of physical problems, most commonly hip dysplasia. I urge all owners of large dogs and any dogs that are having difficulty with this exercise to have their dogs' hips X-rayed before starting serious jumping practice. Some dysplastic dogs jump like gazelles, but many do not, and it is important to know if you have an ability problem as opposed to a motivational or training problem. If your dog is dysplastic, speak to your veterinarian about proceeding with the jumping exercises.

Some dogs have jumping problems because of visual faults, including cataracts and other eye diseases. Again, your vet is the best source of information.

If you have a dog that is physically unable to jump his required heights, you may still be able to show him in fun matches and set the jumps as low as necessary.

Not Jumping in One Direction. Dogs fail this exercise most frequently by not jumping in one direction or the other. Teach your dog to jump no matter where the dumbbell lands, gradually increasing the angle of your throw. There are many different ways to accomplish this. Speak to your instructor.

A dog that climbs the jump will fail this exercise. A dog that merely touches the jump will lose points. If your dog hits the jump hard enough to knock it over, he will also fail. The dog must jump smoothly and confidently.

Some dogs are physically unable to clear the jumps because of physical problems, most commonly hip dysplasia. I urge all owners of large dogs and any dogs that are having difficulty with this exercise to have their dogs' hips X-rayed before starting serious jumping practice.

Dogs fail this exercise most frequently by not jumping in one direction or the other. Teach your dog to jump no matter where the dumbbell lands.

This is not and exercise that you can proof in your backyard. Take your jumps to as many different places as you can when practicing this exercise. If you plan to show indoors, set up your jump next to walls or baby gates.

Common Handling Errors

- *Dropping the dumbbell.*
- *Moving your feet after sending the dog for the dumbbell.*
- *Not throwing the dumbbell at least eight feet beyond the jump.*

Pass

- *If your dog waited for your command.*
- *If your dog left on the first command.*
- *If your dog jumped in both directions and returned with the dumbbell.*

Fail

- *If your dog climbs the jump or hits the jump hard enough to knock it over.*
- *If your dog does not jump in one direction or the other.*
- *If the dog does not bring back the dumbbell.*

I believe that more dogs fail to jump *after* the retrieve than *before,* because the dog will naturally tend to follow the trajectory of the dumbbell and go over the jump on the way out. On the return, there is no such incentive. It is vital that you take your jumps to as many different places as you can when practicing this exercise. Not only will your own jump look different to the dog in different places, but someone else's jump will look totally alien and the dog will not be able to generalize from one set of jumps to another.

This is not an exercise that you can proof in your backyard. Set up your jump in odd places, with strange backgrounds. Have people (or better still, people and dogs) doing interesting things close to the area where you are training. If you plan to show indoors, set up your jump next to walls or baby gates. If you do not have access to different sets of jumps, make your own jump look different by draping a jacket over the top.

Common Handling Errors

Common handling errors for the Retrieve Over the High Jump include the following:

- Dropping the dumbbell.
- Moving your feet after sending the dog for the dumbbell.
- Not throwing the dumbbell at least eight feet beyond the jump.

Pass or Fail?

If the dog waited for your command, left on the first command, jumped in both directions, and returned with the dumbbell, he probably passed. On more than one occasion, a dog has dropped the dumbbell before the return jump, and with no additional command from the handler has realized his error and jumped back over the jump, picked up the dumbbell, and completed the retrieve over the high jump again. Most judges will qualify the dog that does this, although many points will be lost.

Broad Jump

Distance from Jump/Position in Front of Jump

As with the high jump, starting the dog consistently from the same distance may be beneficial, keeping in mind the eight-foot minimum. Some exhibitors prefer to position their dogs to the left of the center of the jump rather than centering the dog in front of the jump. This is supposed to prevent the dog from cutting the right corner when he jumps.

Handler's Position After Leaving the Dog

After leaving the dog, the handler must stand facing the side of the jump, two feet back from it. You may choose to stand anywhere between the low edge of the

For the Broad Jump, starting the dog consistently from the same distance may be beneficial, keeping in mind the eight-foot minimum.

After leaving the dog, the handler must stand facing the side of the jump, two feet back from it.

The handler turns while the dog is in midair and is facing forward as the dog lands.

You must make a ninety-degree turn to your right while the dog is in midair. Do not overturn to compensate for your dog's overly wide return circle.

first board and the high edge of the last board. Practice standing in different spots to see which position allows the dog to sit straight in front without cutting the corner of the jump as he turns. *You must make a ninety-degree turn to your right while the dog is in midair.* Do not overturn to compensate for your dog's overly wide return circle. Many exhibitors whose dogs usually finish to the left teach their dog to finish to the right for this exercise. Larger dogs, especially, may have difficulty finishing to the left in the rather small area between the handler and the jump.

Proofing the Broad Jump

To proof the Broad Jump, make the jump look different to the dog by laying something on the jump or setting the jump at an angle to a wall or fence. Some trainers gradually remove the middle boards to be sure that the dog understands that he must clear the entire distance of the jump.

Different Settings/Different Jumps. The statements made about dogs' initial inability to jump a familiar high jump placed in different settings, or to jump different high jumps, also apply to the broad jump. Make the jump look different to the dog by laying something on the jump or setting the jump at an angle to a wall or fence. Some trainers gradually remove the middle boards to be sure that the dog understands that he must clear the entire distance of the jump, no matter how much space is between the boards.

A dog that cuts the far right corner of the jump will lose points and may even fail. Be certain that your dog does not tour the ring on his way back to you.

Jumping in a Straight Line. The AKC does not require that the dog bisect the jump in a perfectly straight line, but a dog that cuts the far right corner of the jump will lose points and may even fail. Speak to your instructor about ways to teach the dog to jump in a straight line. Be certain that your dog does not tour the ring on his way back to you but instead comes directly to front position at a trot. Have someone acting as judge stand in different positions around the jump and be sure that your dog will not go to the judge to visit or investigate.

Collecting the Dumbbell. Many judges do not have a steward collect the dumbbell from the handler after the high jump but instead take it from the exhibitor and carry it with them during the Broad Jump exercise. If your dog is a retrieving fanatic, have the person playing judge hold the dog's dumbbell in plain sight, and make the appropriate correction if the dog attempts to collect his dumbbell on the way back to you.

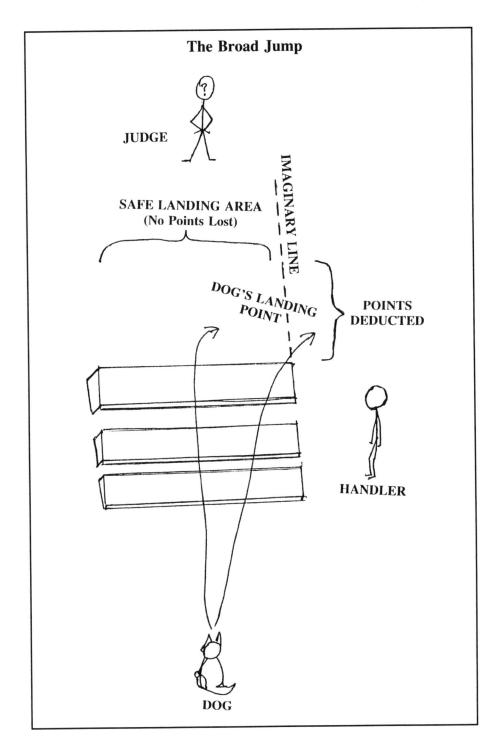

The Broad Jump

JUDGE

SAFE LANDING AREA
(No Points Lost)

IMAGINARY LINE

DOG'S LANDING POINT

POINTS DEDUCTED

HANDLER

DOG

Common Handling Errors

- *Using body English when sending the dog.*
- *Failing to make the turn correctly and smoothly.*
- *Standing too close or too far from the side of the jump.*

Pass

- *If the dog waits for your command.*
- *If the dog clears the jump correctly on your first command.*
- *If the dog returns within arm's reach.*

Fail

- *If the dog knocks over any part of the jump.*
- *If the dog uses the jump for aid.*

Lose Points

- *If the dog touches the jump.*
- *If the dog cuts the right corner.*
- *If the dog returns slowly.*
- *If the dog makes a wide circle rather than returning directly to the handler.*

Common Handling Errors

The most common handling errors on this exercise are:

- Using body English when sending the dog.
- Failing to make the turn correctly and smoothly.
- Standing too close or too far from the side of the jump.

Pass or Fail?

The latest revision of the *Regulations* somewhat muddied the waters on this exercise. It used to be true that a dog had to clear the broad jump with his forelegs to pass. Under the new *Regulations,* the Broad Jump is to be treated like the High Jump, in that knocking over any part of the jump or using the jump for aid (e.g., pushing off the first board) is an automatic zero. Other types of jump touches will be scored at the judge's discretion, costing the team anything from a minor deduction to failure of the exercise.

At the most recent AKC judging seminar I attended, I asked at what point a judge should begin to make deductions for a dog jumping at an angle. I was told to imagine a line extending several feet beyond the right side of the jump. If the dog lands inside that line (see illustration), no points should be deducted, the angle of the jump notwithstanding. The moment the dog lands to the right of that line, deductions may be taken.

Therefore, if the dog waits for your command, clears the jump as described above on your first command, and returns within arm's reach, he will probably pass.

Dogs lose points for touching the jump, cutting the right corner, returning slowly, and making a wide circle rather than returning directly to the handler. A dog that makes an extremely wide return circle in a small ring may find himself in front of the high jump. If he jumps the high jump and still manages to get within the handler's reach without any additional command, he should pass, although he will lose many points. This is a surprisingly common occurrence in the Open ring.

Open Group Exercises

The rules governing the three-minute, out-of-sight Long Sit and five-minute Long Down are essentially the same as for the Novice group exercises. Pay attention to the people on either side of you so that you can find your place in the line before the group returns from its hidden position. Keep track of the time that has elapsed, not to outguess the judge, but to have an idea of when to line up for the return.

At one trial, an exhibitor wandered away from the group and did not notice when the handlers were called back to the ring. The judge was certainly surprised to find one dog left over when the exercise was finished. (A steward was sent in search of the absent-minded exhibitor.)

If a dog bolts from the ring while the handlers are out of sight, or if he shows aggression toward a steward or another dog, the judge or steward will attempt to catch or remove the dog. If this is not possible, the judge will have the handler called back to the ring before the designated time period has elapsed to collect the dog. Again, listen closely to the judge's instructions so that you will know what to do if you return to find only an empty space where you had left your dog. Remember not to correct your dog for changing position on either exercise, no matter how tempted you are to do so.

The criteria for passing or failing are exactly the same as for the Novice group exercises.

The rules governing the three-minute, out-of-sight Long Sit and five-minute Long Down are essentially the same as for the Novice group exercises.

If a dog bolts from the ring while the handlers are out of sight, or if he shows aggression toward a steward or another dog, the judge or steward will attempt to catch or remove the dog. If this is not possible, the judge will have the handler called back to the ring before the designated time period has elapsed to collect the dog.

Do not correct your dog at the end of the exercise.

■

CHAPTER SIX

The Utility Ring

All of the information pertaining to entering the Open ring (see page 42) applies equally to the Utility ring, except that you will report only one jump height.

Individual Exercises

Signal Exercise

Giving Signals

As was explained under the Drop on Recall, AKC *Regulations* describe only the signal for downing the dog. Other signals can be devised at the handler's discretion, with certain restrictions. Signals may be given with the hand and arm only. No additional body movements are permitted except that the handler *may* bend his or her body and knees to give a signal at the dog's eye level when the dog is in heel position. This means that you may bend down to your Chihuahua, but your signal must not touch the dog. You may *not* bend to give a signal to a dog *except* when he is in heel position. Your recall and finish signals must be given with no bending.

Signals must be silent. All signals must consist of a single gesture — not a series of jerky movements around the handler's head and body — and the signaling arm must be returned immediately to a natural position at the handler's side. Observe yourself giving signals in a mirror,

Signals may be given with the hand and arm only. No additional body movements are permitted except that the handler may bend his or her body and knees to give a signal at the dog's eye level when the dog is in heel position. Signals must be silent and must consist of a single gesture.

or have somebody film you to be sure that your signals meet these requirements.

Strive to keep your signals the same each time you give them. It is also advisable to be sure that your signals for the different parts of the exercise appear distinct to the dog. Some exhibitors use a series of nearly identical gestures, which must be confusing to the dog. Check with your instructor.

Handicapped handlers who have limited use of their hands and arms may make arrangements with the judge before they enter the ring to signal with some other part of the body. They should show the judge the signals that they intend to use so that the judge has a basis on which to determine the dog's response.

You may bend to give a signal at the dog's eye level only when the dog is in heel position.

The *Regulations* clearly state that *signals may not be held* or the team will fail the exercise. However, you may want to consider holding a signal for a few seconds if the dog looks away just as you begin a signal. If the dog responds as soon as he looks back at you, the judge may choose to make a very substantial deduction but may pass the dog. This is an individual judgment call that will vary from judge to judge. Similarly, if the dog becomes distracted immediately after the judge has indicated that you are to give a particular signal, you would be wise to wait until the dog looks at you before giving your signal. I can't guarantee that you will pass in either of these situations, but you really have nothing to lose by waiting, and many teams have squeaked by and qualified under these circumstances.

Signals may not be held. However, you may want to consider holding a signal for a few seconds if the dog looks away just as you begin a signal or waiting to give the signal. If the dog responds as soon as he looks back at you, the judge may make a very substantial deduction but may pass the dog.

Proofing the Signal Exercise

Distractions. Once again, dog attention is the key to success in this exercise. Therefore, you must create conditions of distraction under which you can practice and teach the dog to respond no matter what is going on. Once you are sure that the dog understands the signals, do not always wait for him to look at you in training before giving a signal. If he is looking away, proceed to give the signal, then act if he fails to respond. Don't be surprised if the dog responds correctly while looking away from you. Dogs have excellent peripheral (side) vision when they choose to use it.

Dog attention is the key to success in the Signal Exercise. Therefore, you must create distractions under which you can practice and teach the dog to respond no matter what is going on.

Be sure that the dog will tolerate having a person standing behind him, making gestures while he performs the Signal Exercise. I often have my pretend judge stand next to the dog (almost in heel position) and make noisy, exaggerated signal motions while I insist that the dog focus on me. Once I am sure that my dog knows the signals, I will have people and their dogs walk between me and my dog for distraction while I give the signals.

Anticipation. Prevent anticipation by mixing the order of your signals. Turn your back to the dog and signal (unless you use tiny signals given in front of your body). Give the dog a signal, then walk away for a moment

Prevent anticipation by mixing the order of your signals.

Work to keep your dog from moving forward on any signal.

Common Handling Errors

- *Using body English.*
- *Giving verbal commands on the heeling portion.*
- *Holding signals when the dog is watching (and simply not responding).*
- *Taking too many steps forward before obeying the command "Stand your dog."*

Pass

- *If the dog performed the heeling portion adequately.*
- *If the dog waited for and responded to the first signals to stand, stay, down, sit, and come.*
- *If the dog did not move forward more than about a body length while progressing through the first four signals.*

Lose Points

- *If the dog responded slowly to any signal.*
- *If the dog walked forward a few steps.*
- *If you needed to give a verbal command to heel or to finish.*

before giving the next signal. Stand at an angle to the dog, or better still, sit down and give your signals.

Preventing Your Dog from Moving Forward. Work to keep the dog from moving forward on any signal. Most competitive trainers teach their dogs to fold backwards into the down (as opposed to sitting first and then putting the front end down), and to sit from the down by bringing the front feet back without any movement of the rump.

Common Handling Errors

The most common handling errors seen in this exercise are:

- Using body English.
- Giving verbal commands on the heeling portion of the exercise.
- Holding signals when the dog is watching (and simply not responding).
- Taking too many steps forward before obeying the command "Stand your dog."

Pass or Fail?

If the dog performed the heeling portion adequately and then waited for and responded to the first signals to stand, stay, down, sit, and come, and did not move forward more than about a body length while progressing through the first four signals, he probably passed.

If the dog responded slowly to any signal or walked forward a few steps, he will lose points. A verbal command to heel or to finish will result in a substantial deduction but should not cause the dog to fail.

Scent Discrimination

Articles Used

The requirements regarding the scent articles are clearly spelled out in the *Regulations*. Exhibitors use a wide range of objects as well as the ready-made sets that are sold by various pet-supply firms. Baby shoes, tuna cans, rolled leather scraps, and bent spoons have all been used as scent articles. As long as they are no more than six inches long and are clearly numbered, you may use any items that fit the description in the *Regulations*.

Giving the Scent

The handler must use only his or her hands to scent the article. Some judges will permit the handler to begin scenting the first article while the handler and the dog are watching the articles being placed and scented by the steward. Other judges do not permit you to scent the first article until you have turned your back to the article pile.

It is permissible to give the dog the "mark" command or otherwise focus his attention while the steward is laying out the articles. Be sure that you do not touch the dog as you do this. You may choose to give the dog the scent before sending him by touching his nose with your open hand. Some trainers feel that touching the dog's nose overwhelms him with scent and prefer to keep their hands several inches from the dog's nose. Be careful to return your hand to a natural position at your side after giving the scent and before you turn.

The Turn and Send

This exercise begins when the judge takes the article from the handler. Once you say that you are ready and surrender the article, you must *not* touch or speak to your dog until the judge says, "Send your dog." Then, you may give the dog the scent and turn either to the right or the left to face the articles. I advise my students to turn in whichever direction the dog is most likely to give them a good sit at heel. Be certain that you make a complete 180-degree turn.

The dog should stop and sit before you give the retrieve command. If the dog stops but does not sit, wait a second or two and send him anyway. He will lose points but should not fail. If the dog goes before you give the retrieve command, he will receive a zero for having anticipated.

Taking Care of Your Articles

If you will be showing in Utility on consecutive days, you may want to keep the articles used the first day separate from the others to avoid scent contamination. It is permissible to request that the steward keep the used

---

The requirements regarding the scent articles are clearly spelled out in the Regulations. The handler must use only his or her hands to scent the article.

It is permissible to give the dog the "mark" command or otherwise focus his attention while the steward is laying out the articles. Be sure that you do not touch the dog as you do this.

The Scent Discrimination exercise begins when the judge takes the article from the handler. Once you say that you are ready and surrender the article, you must not touch or speak to your dog until the judge says, "Send your dog." Give the dog the scent and turn either to the right or the left to face the articles. Make a complete 180-degree turn.

If you are showing in Utility on consecutive days, keep the articles used the first day separate from the others to avoid scent contamination.

Get in the habit of counting your articles after you come out of the ring. Mark your articles with your name in some inconspicuous place on the inside of the bell section.

articles separate when you hand him or her your article case before entering the ring. Experienced exhibitors carry two extra scent articles to use the second day of a two-show weekend. Some even carry two complete sets of articles. I have three extra articles of each type made when I purchase a set so that I am prepared for a three-show weekend with fresh articles every time.

Get in the habit of counting your articles after you come out of the ring. Sometimes, stewards forget to replace an article, and it is very upsetting to find this out when you are many miles from the show site, having your next training session. It is not a bad idea to mark your articles with your name in some inconspicuous place on the inside of the bell section.

Proofing Scent Discrimination

The judge can place the pile of articles almost anywhere in the ring. Accustom your dog to working articles between the jumps, in the corners, near the table, and next to or in front of either jump.

Placement of Articles. The judge can place the pile of articles almost anywhere in the ring. Accustom your dog to working articles between the jumps (the most popular spot), in the corners, near the table, and next to or in front of either jump. I prefer to use the corner that has the least traffic and therefore the fewest scents. One handler told me that I could not place the articles anywhere but in the center of the ring. When the handler sent his dog for the first article, the dog went out between the jumps and stood there, looking confused. As I failed the dog, I suggested to the exhibitor that he consult the *Regulations,* but he remained convinced that his belief was accurate. I can only hope that he was able to find judges who liked to place the articles between the jumps.

To be sure that your dog will smell only the articles and not lose points for inattention to the task at hand, work where there are other fascinating smells.

Inattention/Tempting Smells. Remember — this exercise is a variation of the Retrieve on the Flat; therefore, use the proofing techniques described in that section. To be sure that your dog will smell only the articles and not lose points for inattention to the task at hand, work where there are other fascinating smells. One of our favorite article-proofing spots is near a lagoon in a park where there are piles of duck and goose droppings. I have also worked articles in a horse pasture and next to a bitch in season.

Dogs That Move Articles. Frequently, dogs will move articles around with their noses, tails, or feet as they search the pile. Sometimes they will kick the correct article a distance away from the pile and then be unable to find it. I teach my dog to continue searching by gradually moving the articles farther and farther apart, until the scented article is as far as three feet from the pile.

Similarly, a dog may kick or pick up and drop a wrong article on top of the correct article. Train him to dig the correct article out from underneath the wrong article. Stand your articles on end rather than laying them flat, and teach the dog that he can still retrieve an article in that position.

Frequently, dogs will move articles around with their noses, tails, or feet as they search the pile. I teach my dog to continue searching by gradually moving the articles farther and farther apart, until the scented article is as far as three feet from the pile. Stand the articles on end.

Continuing the Search. Some dogs make a quick tour of the articles, and if they do not immediately find the scented one, they return to the handler (sometimes with an accusatory look: "You forgot to put the right article out there!"). Insist that the dog continue to search, and make it harder in practice by using two sets of articles. We also proof dogs by having them do their articles together, so that they not only have to check out twenty or more articles but must find the correct (not just the freshest or hottest) scent.

Insist that the dog continue to search, and make it harder in practice by using two sets of articles. We also proof dogs by having them do their articles together.

Small Dogs Outdoors. If you have a small dog and show outdoors, practice having the pile of articles invisible to the dog in tall grass (or over the edge of a hill or curb) so that the dog believes there is something there to find, even if he can't see it.

If you have a small dog, practice having the pile of articles invisible to the dog in tall grass.

Common Handling Errors
A handler will lose points on this exercise for:

- Looking over his or her shoulder to watch the scented article being placed.
- Using excessive body English in sending the dog.
- Attempting to control the dog by facial expression while he is smelling the articles.
- Shuffling his or her feet around after sending the dog.

Common Handling Errors

- *Looking over your shoulder to watch the scented article being placed.*
- *Using excessive body English in sending the dog.*
(Continued on next page)

• *Trying to control the dog by facial expression while he is smelling the articles.*
• *Shuffling your feet around after sending the dog.*

Pass

• *If the dog waited for and then went out on the first command.*
• *If the dog retrieved the correct article and brought it back within arm's reach.*

Lose Points

• *Poor turn and sit.*
• *Dawdling.*
• *Gazing into space.*
• *Sniffing anything but the pile of articles.*
• *Wandering around the ring.*
• *Jumping a jump.*
• *Picking up and putting down a wrong article.*
• *Slow response on any part of the exercise.*

The gloves required for the Directed Retrieve are described as "cotton work gloves may be all white or may have colored cuffs. The most difficult and critical part of this The most difficult and critical part of this exercise is the turn toward the desired glove. Work toward making smooth turns.

Pass or Fail?

If the dog waited for and then went out on the first command, retrieved the right article, and brought it back within arm's reach, he probably passed.

The dog will lose points for a poor turn and sit, for dawdling, for gazing into space, and for sniffing anything but the pile of articles. He may sniff at the articles for any reasonable time without being penalized, however.

Wandering around the ring, or jumping a jump on the way to or from the article pile, will be penalized, as will picking up and putting down a wrong article. The *Regulations* do not specify a penalty for a dog that picks up the correct article, puts it down, smells the other articles again, and then retrieves the original correct article, but some judges consider this the same as dropping a dumbbell and will make a deduction.

As in the Retrieve on the Flat, a slow response on any part of this exercise will be penalized.

Directed Retrieve

The Gloves

The gloves required for this exercise are described as "cotton work gloves," which are predominantly white. The gloves may be all white or may have colored cuffs. If there is a light-colored floor with glare from a window or light, the all-white glove may not be as visible as the dark-cuffed glove. Some owners of toy dogs manage to find children's work gloves. The *Regulations* do not mention the size of the gloves. All gloves should be clean.

Some handlers try to make the gloves more visible to the dog by starching them into odd configurations so that they will not lie flat. Most judges are alert to this trick and will either have the steward flatten the gloves or require the handler to supply gloves that comply with the *Regulations*.

The Turn Toward the Desired Glove

The most difficult and critical part of this exercise is the turn toward the desired glove. You may turn to the right or the left for any glove. You will lose points for underturning or overturning and can also make the retrieve more difficult for the dog. Work with your instructor or your mirror to learn to make smooth turns.

Directional Signals

This exercise is the only retrieving exercise in which a signal is required by the *Regulations*. Two signals are permitted on this exercise. In the first, the handler thrusts or swings the left arm forward in a pointing motion, simultaneously giving the retrieve command, and then immediately returns the arm to his or her side (see the photo). In the second, the handler holds the arm steady along the right side of the dog's head while pointing in the correct direction, then gives the retrieve command immediately.

Judges should penalize or fail a handler who brings his or her arm alongside the dog's head, pauses a moment, then thrusts the arm forward while giving the retrieve command, because this is not the single gesture called for in the *Regulations*. Some trainers prefer the steady signal and send (which is more like the "mark" exercise used in retrieving trials, on which this exercise is sup-

Two signals are permitted in the Directed Retrieve. In the first, the handler thrusts or swings the left arm forward in a pointing motion, simultaneously giving the retrieve command, and then immediately returns the arm to his or her side. In the second, the arm is held steady along the right side of the dog's head while pointing in the correct direction, then the retrieve command is given immediately.

Left: You do not have to bend your knees to give the dog the direction for the glove. Right: The dog should be in motion as the signal is completed.

posedly based), because it permits them to wait a second or two before sending the dog. This can be an advantage if the dog initially focused on an incorrect glove, because it allows him to correct himself before he is sent. However, if the handler waits more than one or two seconds to send the dog, the judge will begin to deduct points and may even fail the dog.

Proofing the Directed Retrieve

The trickiest parts of this exercise are making good turns and getting the dog to take the direction.

Making Good Turns. Because we cannot all consistently make good turns (dogs included), many trainers face the middle glove and use the hand and arm to send the dog for one of the corner gloves. They also use a different name for each glove ("Right," "Left," or "One," "Two," and "Three").

Taking the Direction. To force the dog to focus on the direction that you are giving him rather than on the first glove that he happens to see, try hiding the gloves. Once the dog understands the basics of this exercise, face him toward the edge of a hill or a curb (preferably not on a busy street). Show him the glove and drop it out of his line of vision over the edge of the hill or curb. Then go back and send him to retrieve the hidden glove. Once he catches on, hide all three gloves. If you want to make this especially tough, when the dog is accustomed to having the three gloves hidden and making a correct retrieve, expose one of the gloves and send him for a hidden one.

Other proofing activities are identical to those for the Retrieve on the Flat.

Common Handling Errors

Common handling errors for the Directed Retrieve are:

- Giving the dog the wrong direction by inadvertently swinging your arm wide when giving the signal.
- Waiting more than one or two seconds before sending the dog.

Because we cannot all consistently make good turns (dogs included), many trainers face the middle glove and use the hand and arm to send the dog for one of the corner gloves. They also use a different name for each glove.

To force the dog to focus on the direction that you are giving him rather than on the first glove that he happens to see, try hiding the gloves.

Common Handling Errors

- *Giving the dog the wrong direction by inadvertently swinging your arm wide when giving the signal.*
- *Waiting more than one or two seconds before sending the dog.*
- *Over- or underturning.*
- *Shuffling your feet to help the dog get into a better position.*
- *Moving out of place on the turn.*

- Over- or underturning.
- Shuffling your feet to help the dog get into a better position.
- Moving out of place on the turn. The turn must be performed as a pivot, with the handler in the exact same spot at the beginning and the end (although facing a different direction).

Pass or Fail?

In addition to all of the penalties pertinent to the Retrieve on the Flat, in this particular exercise the dog must go *directly* to the correct glove or he will fail. If the dog is sent for glove number two, for instance, and first goes to number one, and then moves across to the correct glove and retrieves it, he will not receive a qualifying score. Otherwise, scoring for this exercise is identical to the Retrieve on the Flat.

Moving Stand and Examination

This new exercise introduced in 1989 is an improvement over the group Stand for Examination in terms of variety and spectator interest but is much more demanding of the handler. I advise my students to begin the heeling portion with a verbal command in order to distinguish this exercise from the Signal Exercise.

The tricky part is to give a good "stand/stay" command and signal, especially to a small dog. You may give both the command and signal, but you may not pause while you do so, nor may you "change your manner of walking." Teach your small dog to look up for this signal, or to respond well to the voice command, and do not bend to give the signal.

Be consistent in how many steps you take after standing the dog. The average person will cover the ten- to twelve-foot distance in four or five steps. You may turn either direction to face your dog for the examination.

Because the dog is not called to a front sit, your hands do not need to be hanging at your sides (as in a Recall) when you call the dog to heel. You may give both a command and signal to call the dog to heel position,

Pass

- *See Retrieve on the Flat.*
- *If the dog goes directly to the correct glove.*

Fail

- *If the dog does not retrieve the correct glove.*
- *If the dog does not go directly to the glove.*

Begin the heeling portion with a verbal command in order to distinguish this exercise from the Signal Exercise. The tricky part is to give a good "stand/stay" command and signal, especially to a small dog.

When standing the dog on the Moving Stand, the handler must not change body position or her manner of walking.

and he may go to your left or right, as long as he is moving smartly.

Proofing the Moving Stand and Examination

Anticipation. Many dogs anticipate the stand, stopping on the judge's verbal command before the handler has given the command/signal. To proof against this, have someone give you two or three commands to stand your dog while you are heeling, and make an appropriate correction if the dog stops or slows down. If you always train alone, try saying, "Stand your dog" as you are walking, and do not allow the dog to react (obviously,

Many dogs anticipate the stand, stopping on the judge's verbal command before the handler has given the command/signal. To proof against this, have someone give you two or three commands to stand your dog while you are heeling, and make an appropriate correction if the dog stops or slows down.

if you are going to use this for proofing, it is not a good idea to use the word "stand" as your actual command word).

Differences in Commands. Be sure to teach the dog the difference between your command to sit in front and your command to go directly to heel. Use two very distinct words. After all, this part of the exercise was devised to test whether the dog was paying attention to the handler's command, or was mechanically returning to front position every time he was called.

Teach your dog the difference between your command to sit in front and your command to go directly to heel. Use two very distinct words.

The Examination. The proofing for the examination is exactly the same as that for the Novice Stand for Examination, except that you must be certain that the dog will tolerate having all parts of his body touched. Have people lift the dog's ears and tail, touch the feet, and press firmly on the shoulders and chest. If you have a dog with a tightly curled tail (a Pug, a Keeshond, a Basenji), insist that he tolerate having his tail uncurled by a stranger.

You must be certain that your dog will tolerate having all parts of his body touched.

Stance. Since dogs do not always stop in a perfectly square stance on this exercise, practice having the dog stand in awkward positions while he is being examined, and do not permit movement of so much as a toenail. After a few of these uncomfortable experiences, many dogs learn to come into a square stance on their own.

Since dogs do not always stop in a perfectly square stance on this exercise, practice having the dog stand in awkward positions while he is being examined, and do not permit movement of so much as a toenail.

Common Handling Errors

Common handling errors for the Moving Stand and Examination include:

- Giving a command and signal on the initial heeling portion (you may use one or the other, *not* both).
- Slowing down, pausing, or bending while giving the stand/stay.
- Walking more or less than the prescribed ten to twelve feet.
- Giving a poor signal/command for the dog to come to heel.

Common Handling Errors

- *Giving a command and signal on the initial heeling portion.*
- *Slowing down, pausing, or bending while giving the stand/stay.*
- *Walking more or less than the prescribed ten to twelve feet.*
- *Giving a poor signal/command for the dog to come to heel.*

Pass

- *If the dog heels well.*
- *If the dog stands on the command/signal and remains standing throughout the exam without moving more than a body length.*
- *If the dog comes within arm's reach on your first command/ signal.*

Fail

- *If the dog growls or displays his teeth.*
- *If you are flagrant enough in pausing or in using body English.*

Lose Points

- *If a dog sits in front rather than returning to heel position.*

The most difficult feature of Directed Jumping from the dog's point of view is the send-away. The idea of going away from the handler in a straight line is a very abstract concept.

Pass or Fail?

As in the Novice stand, there is a lot of latitude as to what constitutes "displaying fear or resentment" during the examination. A dirty look (and some dogs are particularly good at looking disgusted while being forced to tolerate strange hands on their bodies), or dropping the head as the judge approaches, should not cost any points. Beyond that, it is up to the judge. Certainly a growl or display of teeth will not only earn you a zero but should get you excused from the ring.

If the dog heels reasonably well, stands on the command/signal, remains standing throughout the exam without moving more than a body length, and comes within arm's reach on your first command/signal, he should pass.

A dog that sits in front rather than returning to heel position should lose many points but should not fail. The *Regulations* do not require a zero for the handler pausing or using body English to give the stand/stay; however, if you are flagrant enough in overdoing this behavior, a judge would be within his or her rights to fail you for giving an extra command to the dog.

Directed Jumping

The Send-Away

The most difficult feature of this exercise from the dog's point of view is the send-away. The idea of going away from the handler in a straight line, especially when there is no bird scent (which lures the field dog forward) is a very abstract concept. When the *Regulations* were changed recently, the Moving Stand was inserted between the Directed Retrieve and the Directed Jumping. Previously, many dogs would do their go-outs to the corner from which they had retrieved the glove. Some handlers would go through elaborate machinations to try to be certain that they would be assigned the center glove (telling the judge that they had a sudden stomach upset, or simply being unavailable for their turn if they didn't think that they would be given the center glove). It was hoped that separating the two exercises would eliminate this behavior, and to some extent it has. In spite of the change, some dogs continue to do crooked go-outs. I will discuss

Left: This is an unacceptable signal, using the entire upper body to give the direction. The handler will certainly receive a substantial deduction and could be failed for using this much body English. Right: A good Directed Jumping signal, using only the arm to give the direction.

this problem in the proof-training suggestions that follow later.

If your dog does not go out the required minimum distance of ten feet past the jump, but does stop and sit, the judge may tell you to call him to prevent a possible injury from attempting to jump without sufficient take-off room. Or, you may choose to call him regardless of the judge's direction, because he has already failed. If your dog goes out on the send-away portion of this exercise and does not sit, do not give a second command (unless he has already failed a previous exercise), because he may still qualify. Most judges will wait a few seconds to see if the dog will sit, then will indicate over which jump he is to jump. Dogs that anticipate the turn or the

If your dog goes out on the send-away portion of this exercise and does not sit, do not give a second command, because he may still qualify.

sit will lose points but will not fail if they have gone the required minimum distance. On rare occasions, a dog will stop and sit facing the ring barrier, without turning to face his handler. Regulations call for the dog to have his attention on his handler, so this would require a penalty.

The "Sit" Command

You must give your sit command to the dog when he is at a point about twenty feet past the jumps.

You must give your sit command to the dog when he is at a point about twenty feet past the jumps. At an indoor show, this is usually the front edge of the mat laid across the back edge of the ring. At an outdoor trial, you will not have any such marker. You must practice locating that spot in training. If the dog does very fast go-outs (one judge described a dog that seemed to "materialize at the other end of the ring"), you must train him to respond immediately to your sit command. A fast-moving dog may not end up sitting at the exact twenty-foot mark, but he *should* immediately begin to respond to the command given when he is at the twenty-foot mark. If the dog does not respond, but stops because he has reached the ring barrier, the judge should make a deduction. A dog that sniffs the ring barrier (looking for a training treat) will also receive a deduction.

Commands for Jumps

You may wish to use a different command for each jump to help the dog to choose the correct jump. Your jump signal should be given simultaneously with your verbal command. Be careful to use only your hand and arm to signal; do not make obvious head movements, bend your body, or move your feet.

You may wish to use a different command for each jump to help the dog to choose the correct jump. Your jump signal should be given simultaneously with your verbal command. Be careful to use only your hand and arm to signal; do not make obvious head movements, bend your body, or move your feet. You are not required to give both the signal and verbal command and may use only one if it is beneficial to your dog. Again, as in the Signal Exercise, you may choose to risk holding your jump signal for a few extra seconds if the dog hesitates or appears to be trying to decide which jump to take. You may still qualify but will, of course, lose some points.

Turns

The handler may turn while the dog is in midair to line him or herself up for the dog's return. You are not required to turn, but most trainers believe that it assists the dog in making a good sit in front. Be sure not to overturn or to move your feet around to accommodate a dog that is making a wide return circle.

Proofing the Directed Jumping
Several parts of this exercise require proofing.

Straight, Full-Length Go-Outs/Distractions. A straight, full-length go-out is hard for most dogs. To avoid the glove/go-out confusion mentioned earlier, I train my dogs (once they clearly understand both exercises) to do go-outs over first one, then a myriad of gloves, so that they disassociate the glove retrieve from the go-out. It is also important that the dog not be distracted or intimidated by things happening beyond the go-out point (spectators or competitors and their dogs sitting behind the ring barrier, or having another ring adjacent to the far side of the ring barrier). You must use your ingenuity to set up these types of distractions in training and insist that the dog go the full length no matter what is happening.

If you train your dog to do go-outs to baby gates and are planning to travel to exhibit in other areas of the country, be aware that many areas use only ropes as ring enclosures, and train your dog accordingly. Be sure that your dog will do go-outs to a blank wall or to a wall with doors or other distracting elements in it.

Crooked or Short Go-Outs. Every dog that competes in Utility for any length of time will eventually do a crooked or short go-out. Therefore, you must train your dog to jump either jump from any point in the ring, keeping in mind the safety of jumping a dog from less than a ten-foot distance.

I had carefully trained one of my dogs to take either jump from the opposite corner. At our second Utility show, he did a poor go-out and wound up in the corner opposite the jump that the judge had been giving first. Thinking to do us a favor, the judge changed her pattern and designated the jump closest to the dog. The dog, however, was not to be fooled and proudly crossed the ring to take the far jump. The moral of this story is, be

The handler may turn while the dog is in midair to line him or herself up for the dog's return. Be sure not to overturn or to move your feet around to accommodate a dog that is making a wide return circle.

A straight, full-length go-out is hard for most dogs. To avoid the glove/ go-out confusion, I train my dogs to do go-outs over first one, then a myriad of gloves, so that they disassociate the glove retrieve from the go-out.

You must use ingenuity to set up distractions in training and insist that the dog go the full length no matter what is happening.

Every dog that competes in Utility for any length of time will eventually do a crooked or short go-out. Therefore, you must train your dog to jump either jump from any point in the ring, keeping in mind the safety of jumping a dog from less than a ten-foot distance.

sure that your dog will take *either* jump from *either* corner.

Bar Jumps. The bar jump is especially difficult for some dogs. The stripes that make it more visible to us, in my opinion, make it harder for the dog to see against most backgrounds. Furthermore, the dog must look upward to locate the bar (except for those breeds that jump only once their shoulder height), making it even more difficult. Proof this part of the exercise by deliberately making the bar hard to find. Set it against walls, under trees, or alongside other visual distractions. If your dog continues to have problems with the bar, have his eyes checked by your veterinarian. Even moderate eye problems can severely affect the dog's performance of this part of the Directed Jumping.

Common Handling Errors

Common handling errors for the Directed Jumping are:

- Letting the dog go all the way to the ring barrier.
- Giving a second command if your dog does not sit.
- Using body English to give a signal.
- Turning incorrectly (only when the dog is in midair.)
- Overturning to compensate for your dog.
- Bending your knees to give the go-out signal (*unless* you have a small dog).

Pass or Fail?

In order to qualify, the dog must do the following things for each half of the exercise:

- Wait for and then go away on the first command.
- Go out between the jumps (if he jumps on the way out, he will fail).
- Go at least ten feet past the jumps, stop and wait for the direction to be given, jump as directed, and return within reach of the handler.

If he ticks either jump, he will lose points, but if he knocks the bar off, he will fail. Dogs also lose points for slow response on any part of the exercise, failing to go the full twenty feet away, not stopping in the center of the ring, and failing to return directly to the handler. The farther the dog stops from the ideal centered, twenty-foot mark, the more points he will lose.   ■

CHAPTER SEVEN

Reaping the Rewards

The Pleasure of Honest Handling

There is nothing quite as fulfilling as setting a goal, working hard to achieve it, and succeeding. The nice thing about the sport of obedience is that not only do you receive public acknowledgement of your success in the form of certificates, ribbons, trophies, and ratings, but you also wind up with a dog that is a delightful pet and with whom you have a deep, mutually beneficial understanding. Those few exhibitors who "nudge" the rules, and those who frankly cheat, even if they are not caught, rob themselves of some of this pleasure and cheapen the sport for everyone.

While exhibitors who cheat may fool some judges, they cannot fool themselves or fellow exhibitors. They may gain a number of additional trophies for their collections, but they will eventually lose the respect of the obedience community. It has been my experience that dishonest exhibitors come to be ostracized by that community.

Giving Back to the Sport

If you have derived pleasure from training and showing in obedience, consider putting forth some effort to making the sport accessible to others. Join an obedience club or an all-breed club (they always need obedience enthusiasts), and volunteer to help put on their next match or show. Offer to take on one of the many tasks involved. Make yourself available to judge at a local fun match. (This is how many AKC judges get started.) Help the club run its training classes, if any.

The nice thing about the sport of obedience is that not only do you receive public acknowledgement of your success in the form of certificates, ribbons, trophies, and ratings, but you also wind up with a dog that is a delightful pet and with whom you have a deep, mutually beneficial understanding.

If you have derived pleasure from training and showing, consider putting forth some effort to making the sport accessible to others. Join an obedience club or an all-breed club, and volunteer to help put on their next match or show. You don't have to be an expert trainer to participate in these activities. Use your imagination to make the skills you have acquired bring pleasure and information to others.

Remain flexible. The successful trainers and exhibitors enjoy the sport of obedience as a learning experience, an opportunity for personal growth.

Your trained dog can also be the centerpiece for discussions about responsible pet ownership with friends or public groups. Some exhibitors give presentations at local schools or work with Scout groups. Your titled dog may be eligible to become a Therapy Dog, to be used to bring joy to elderly and/or handicapped residents in nursing homes or other institutions. Check around in your area to see if training classes are offered for the disabled and their dogs; extra hands are always welcome. You may volunteer to help at a local guide-dog school or at one of the new places that train dogs for the hearing impaired and the physically disabled. You will probably not do any actual training of such dogs but may be needed to help care for them, to socialize puppies, etc. The local Humane Society also has many uses for knowledgeable volunteers.

You don't have to be an expert trainer or have a dog that always scores 198 to participate in these activities. A person who has trained and shown even one dog to a C.D. has many times the knowledge of the average pet owner. Use your imagination to make the skills you have acquired bring pleasure and information to others.

There are other activities in which you can participate with an obedience-trained dog. Agility is becoming very popular and requires a dog to be under verbal control, to take directions, to jump, and to stay. The AKC recently instituted Canine Good Citizenship tests to encourage the general public to give their dogs basic obedience training. A dog trained to a C.D. level should pass this test easily.

There are a number of non-AKC events for dogs that are able to earn high scores, including the regional and national Gaines competitions, the World Series (canine version), and various regional competitions such as the Western Interstate Obedience Competition. For more information about these events, consult *Front and Finish,* or ask an experienced exhibitor who shows in Open B and Utility in your area.

Finally, *remain flexible.* The most successful trainers are not the ones who have success with only one dog, and who eventually disappear because they could never achieve the same success with subsequent dogs. Nor are they the people who discard dogs like used Kleenex when the dogs do not win. The successful trainers and exhibitors enjoy the sport of obedience as a learning experience, an opportunity for personal growth. Whether each new dog is a big winner or merely qualifies, training him is a fresh challenge. Every year brings new friends and new relationships, as well as new ideas. Obedience is a sport for everyone, because everyone can be a winner, canine and human alike.

Obedience is a sport for everyone, because everyone can be a winner, canine and human alike.

∎

A P P E N D I X

PHOTO ACKNOWLEDGEMENTS

I extend my sincere thanks to all of the people and their dogs who posed endlessly (and sometimes repeatedly) for these photos. You have my deepest appreciation. Special thanks to Kent and Donna Dannen and Joanne Bartley for the magnificent cover photo and all of the Samoyed photos. A reviewer of the original *Best Foot Forward* noted that there were some unusual breeds illustrating the book and that most of them were breed champions. That was not an accident. I hope to encourage more people to try obedience with non-Goldens, Border Collies, Poodles, etc. This time, I tried for even more variety!

Cover photo: Joanne L. Bartley and Ch. Wind River Talkeetna Karibou CD (Samoyed) owned by Kent and Donna Dannen. Joanne and Karibou also appear on pages 46, 49, and 58.

Page 6: Joni Freshman, DVM and Ch. Charsar Zephyr Sierra CD, TT, HT (Belgian Tervuren).

Page 15: Richard G. Cook and Nancy Johnson Cook and OTCh Leolair's Aldebaran D'Hyades (Shetland Sheepdog)

Page 22: Barbera V. Curtis and Ch. Beschutzer Fire of Kassander UDT (Australian Terrier). "Kass" is also seen on pages 69 and 76 with his friend Debbie Kujaczynski.

Page 25: Joanne Peterson and Busy B's Kitfox UD (Pembroke Welsh Corgi).

Page 36: Kathy Spahr and Ch. Jigsaw Puzzle of the Pines CD (Pug). Kathy and "Doozer" also appear on pages 43 and 70.

Page 55: Joanne L. Bartley and Ch. Snowflower Spun Sugar CD (Samoyed), co-owned with the Dannens. "Spinner" is also seen on page 73.

Page 56: Deborah S. Garfield and Ch. Tramore More Often Than Not CD (Irish Setter). Judge played by Debbie Kujaczynski. Deb and "Mari" also appear on page 87. "Mari" is seen on pages 69, 70, 73, and 76.

Page 61: Linda Hart and Ch. Tru Blu Bei Under My Spell UD (Silky Terrier). Linda and "Bea" also appear on pages 64 and 70. I hope by the time this is published, Bea will have earned those last three elusive points to become the only Ch-OTCh Silky Terrier.

Page 61: L. T. Ward and Ch. Bonnie's Bane Tarroo CDX (Bull Terrier). Also seen on pages 66, 67, 76, and 77.

Page 62: Rachel B. Lachow and Ch. Shema's Nefer-Eleni, CD, FCh. (Pharoah Hound). Rachel and/or "Eleni" are also seen on pages 69, 70, 73, and 76.

Page 63: Kathy Heun and Ch. Broken Oaks Gideon V. Arjana CD (Bernese Mountain Dog).

Page 76: Karen J. Humm and Ch. Grianan's Cailin DeMasque CD (Irish Wolfhound), L. T. Ward with Bull Terrier "Bane" and Beth Ward with Ch. Rustic's

127

Panda Bear CD. This crew also appear on page 77.

Page 81: I had to get in a picture of my old friend, Ch. and OTCh Fern Hill Act One TD (Belgian Tervuren), who also appears on page 99.

Page 91: Ch. Maldolph's Baron Von Zureeg CDX (Keeshond) owned by the author and Sue Riegel.

Page 113: Henry Fellerman and Ch. Rocky Mountain High Hannibal CDX (Kuvasz).

Page 116: Pat Kadel and OTCh Boulder's Bubbling Benjy (Wire Fox Terrier). Pat and "Benjy" also appear on page 119.

DOG-TRAINING EQUIPMENT THROUGH THE MAIL

Acme Machine Co., 2901 Fremont Avenue South, Minneapolis, MN 55408. Phone: 1-800-332-2472. This company sells dumbbells and different types of jumps. Write or call for catalogue.

Doctors Foster and Smith, Inc., 509 Shepard Street, Rhinelander, WI 54501. Phone: 1-800-826-7206. This company sells collars and leashes, dumbbells, and many other pet supplies including vaccines and medical products. Catalogue available.

Hoadleygold, Inc., Rt. 3, Box 30, Monticello, FL 32344. These folks are obedience people and sell lightweight jumps, plastic dumbbells, and baby gates (for setting up rings or practicing go-outs). Write for brochure.

J-B Wholesale Pet Supplies, 289 Wagaraw Road, Hawthorne, NJ 07506. Phone: 1-800-526-0388. This company sells all kinds of dog supplies and books, as well as collars, leashes, and dumbbells. Catalogue available.

J and J Dog Supplies, P.O. Box 1517, Galesburg, IL 61402. The first company to cater to obedience people. J and J sells all types of collars, leashes, jumps, dumbbells, scent articles, and other things that obedience people crave. Write for catalogue.

Paul's Obedience Shop, 1213 Little River Drive, Elizabeth City, NC 27909. The name says it all: dumbbells, scent articles, leashes, and collars. Catalogue available.

R.C. Steele, 1989 Transit Way, Box 910, Brockport, NY 14420-0910, or 1-800-872-3773. Another general pet merchandise catalogue, selling everything from toys to crates to collars. Prices are low, but there is a minimum order of $50.00. Catalogue available.

Sylvia's Tack Box, 4333 11th Street A, Moline, IL 61265. Specializes in items for toy and small dogs.

Wholesale Pet USA, P.O. Box 9281, Colorado Springs, CO 80932, or 1-800-444-0404. Yet another general merchandise catalogue, with a $50.00 minimum order. Write for catalogue.

Zerick Co., Rt. 1, Box 1547, Walland, TN 37886. Sells jumps and "Mutt Mats," washable dog rugs.

IMPORTANT ADDRESSES

American Kennel Club (AKC)
51 Madison Avenue
New York, New York 10010

Organizations That Award Titles to Mixed-Breed Dogs and Non-Registerable Purebreds

NEON (New England Obedience News)
All-American Titles
70 Medford St., P.O. Box 105
Chicopee, MA 01020

American Mixed Breed Obedience Registry
205 First St. SW
New Prague, MN 56071

Mixed Breed Dog Club of America
1937 Seven Pines Drive
St. Louis, MO 63146

Licensed Superintendents

Antypas, William G.
P.O. Box 7131
Pasadena, CA 91109

Bradshaw, Jack
P.O. Box 7303
Los Angeles, CA 90022

Brown, Norman E.
P.O. Box 2566
Spokane, WA 99220

Crowe, Thomas J.
P.O. Box 22107
Greensboro, NC 27420

Houser, M. Helen
P.O. Box 420
Quakertown, PA 18951

Matthews, Ace H.
P.O. Box 06150
Portland, OR 97206

Onofrio, Jack
P.O. Box 25764
Oklahoma City, OK 73125

Peters, Bob
P.O. Box 579
Wake Forest, NC 27587

Rau, James A.
P.O. Box 6898
Reading, PA 19610

Roberts, B. Jeannie
P.O. Box 4658
Federal Way, WA 98063

Sleeper, Kenneth A.
P.O. Box 828
Auburn, IN 46706

Wilson, Nancy
8307 E. Camelback Rd.
Scottsdale, AZ 85251

Barbara Handler is an obedience judge, trainer, and exhibitor whose involvement in the sport began in 1972 when her first dog earned his CD. Since that time, her dogs have earned thirty-two additional titles, including several breed championships (some with group placements), three TDs, and two OTChs. Her dogs have been multi-High in Trial winners and have been in the top positions in national ratings systems. She has run training classes since 1973 and has also directed obedience classes for the physically disabled. Barbara is approved to judge all obedience classes.

Her involvement in the sport has extended to the field of journalism with several articles appearing in such local and national publications as *Front & Finish,* the *AKC Gazette,* and *Dog World.* She has written a training book titled *Positively Obedient — Good Manners for the Family Dog,* which offers non-violent, inducive methods for pet owners to learn to control their dogs.

Barbara is employed as a supervising counselor with the Colorado Division of Rehabilitation and in this capacity works with the disabled.